D1104808

The Ultimate
Hungarian Cookbook

111 Dishes From Hungary To Cook Right Now

Slavka Bodic

Introduction

For eons, traditional Hungarian cuisine has been acclaimed for its unique, exotic, and irresistible tastes and aromas. The rich culinary culture of Hungary has gained many influences from all parts of Europe, and those inspirations are directly reflected through the diversity of flavors that you'll find in the Hungarian entrees, desserts, drinks, breakfasts, etc. The great benefit about Hungarian food is that it not only tastes great, but it's also rich in healthy and nutritious ingredients. It offers your number of unique combinations of fruits, vegetables, grains, beans, legumes, seafood, and meat, etc. If you're as curious about Hungarian Cuisine as I was before getting to know it and you want to explore all its different flavors, then this cookbook offers a perfect read for you!

The *Ultimate Hungarian Cookbook* will introduce to Hungarian cuisine and its culinary culture in a practical and personal way. It delivers a variety of Hungarian recipes in one place. The book is great for all those who are always keen to cook healthy food and want to try new and unique flavors. With the help of this Hungarian cuisine cookbook, you can create a complete Hungarian menu at home, or you can try all the special Hungarian recipes on your special occasions and celebrations.

In this cookbook, you'll find popular Hungarian meals and the ones that you might not have heard of. From nourishing breakfasts to all of the vegetable soups, the exotic desserts, drinks, main dishes, and Hungarian salads, etc., you can find them all. And all these recipes are created in such a simple way that those who aren't even familiar with the Hungarian culture, food, and language can still try and cook them at home without facing much hassle.

Hungarian culinary culture and cuisine are full of surprises. You might never expect to have a mix of western and eastern cuisines all in one place, but Hungarian food makes that possible with its Balkan and European Influences. So if you want to bring all those flavors to your dinner table, then give this book a thorough read, and you'll find all the answers in one place.

What you can find in this Cookbook:
- Insights about the Hungarian Cuisine
- Facts About Hungary
- Delectable Hungarian Breakfast Recipes
- Tempting Sides and Appetizers
- Delicious Soup Recipes
- Tasty Main Dishes
- Iconic Hungarian desserts
- Classic Hungarian Drinks

Let's try all these Hungarian recipes and recreate a complete menu to celebrate the amazing Hungarian flavors and rich aromas.

Table Of Contents

INTRODUCTION 3

WHY HUNGARIAN CUISINE? 9

HUNGARY 11

BREAKFAST 13

Hungarian Crepes (Magyar Palacsinta)........................ 14
Paprika Tomatoes with Eggs (Shakshuka)................... 16
Hungarian Scrambled Eggs (Magyaros Tojásrántotta) ... 18
Potato and Sausage Casserole (Rakottkrumpli)............ 20
Hungarian Mushroom Omelet 21
Hungarian Omelet.. 23
Potato Tofu Casserole 24
Hungarian Apple Pancakes (Almás-Fahéjas Palacsinta) ... 26
Hungarian Cauliflower Potato Casserole 27
Pull-Apart Cake with Apricot Jam (Aranygaluska)......... 28
Hungarian Kifli.. 30

APPETIZERS AND SNACKS 31

Hungarian Nut Roll 32
Pickled Sweet Peppers 34
Hunza Bread 35
Hungarian Fried Lángos 36
Hungarian Cheese Spread (Körözött) 37
Peanut Butter Bites 38
Hungarian Cheese Scones (Pogacsa).......................... 39
Hungarian Stuffed Cabbage 40

SALADS 41

Chalamade Cabbage Salad 42
Hungarian Pepper, Tomato And Cucumber Salad 43
Hungarian Salad 44
Sour Cream Cucumber Salad (Téjfélés Uborka Saláta) ... 45
Hungarian Olive Salad 46
Hungarian Cucumber Salad 47
Hungarian Chopped Salad 48
Hungarian Potato Salad 49
Hungarian Style Lettuce Salad 51

SOUPS 52

FISHERMAN'S SOUP (HALASZLE) 53
GOOSE GIBLET STOCK 54
BEAN SOUP A LA JOKAI (JOKAI BABLEVES) 55
SOUSES SOUP (KORHELYLEVES) 56
PALOC SOUP (PALÓCLEVES) 57
HUNGARIAN KOHLRABI SOUP (KARALABE LEVES) 59
HUNGARIAN KOHLRABI CHICKEN SOUP (ÚJHÁZI) 60
HUNGARIAN MUSHROOM SOUP 62
HUNGARIAN LENTIL SOUP 63
HUNGARIAN CHERRY SOUP (MEGGYLEVES) 64
HUNGARIAN CHICKEN SOUP (HÚSLEVES) 65
STRAWBERRY SOUP 66
HAM GREEN BEAN SOUP 67

MAIN DISHES 69

HUNGARIAN GOULASH 70
CHICKEN PAPRIKASH 71
SAUERKRAUT STUFFED CABBAGE 72
HUNGARIAN SHORT RIBS 74
HUNGARIAN-STYLE GREEN BEANS 75
BEEF PAPRIKASH WITH FIRE-ROASTED TOMATOES 76
GRANDMA SCHWARTZ'S ROULADEN 77
BUTTERNUT GOULASH 78
KOHLRABI AND EGG NOODLES 79
BLAZING BRISKET 80
HUNGARIAN LECSO 81
HUNGARIAN CHOPPED LIVER 82
VEAL PAPRIKASH 83
HUNGARIAN PORK CHOPS 84
CABBAGE BALUSHKA 85
HUNGARIAN LAMB GOULASH 86
HUNGARIAN EGG BARLEY 87
HUNGARIAN NOODLE DISH 88
HUNGARIAN STEW (PORKOLT) 89
BUDAPEST CHICKEN PAPRIKASH 90
PASTA WITH COTTAGE CHEESE (TUROS CSUSZA) 91
GULYAS LEVES 92
PAPRIKASH 93
HUNGARIAN STUFFED PEPPERS 94
CRUMBED POTATO CASSEROLE 95
HUNGARIAN PORK STEW (SERTÉS PAPRIKÁS) 96

Hungarian Green Pea Stew 97
Minced Beef Goulash 98
Hungarian Braided White Bread 99
Sweet Potato and Egg Casserole 100
Zucchini Squash with Dill (Tokfozelek) 101
Paprika Foie Gras on Toast (Paprikás Libamáj) 102
Hunters' Stew (Vada's) 103
Schnitzel (Rántott Hús) 104
Hungarian Pork Stew (Borsos Tokany) 105
Hungarian Paprika Rice 106
Hungarian Tripe Stew (Pacal Porkolt) 107
Hungarian Paprika Potatoes (Paprikás Krumpli) 108
Rice Pilaf with Pork and Vegetables 109
Meat Jelly Aspic (Kocsonya) 110
Hungarian Meatloaf (Stefánia Szelet) 111
Cholent 113
Hungarian Flaky Scones 114

DESSERTS 115
Gerbeaud Cake 116
Hungarian Cream Puffs 118
Hungarian Cookie Bars 119
Hungarian Dobosh Torte 120
Zserbo Szelet 122
Hungarian Apricot Kolaches 124
Chimney Cake 125
Hungarian Walnut Rolls 126
Hungarian Pastry 127
Hungarian Christmas Cake (Beigli) 128
Plum Dumplings (Szilvás Gombóc) 130
Raspberry Cream Roulade (Malna Piskotatekercs) 131
Vanilla Custard Cake 133
Apple Poppy Seed Pastry (Flódni) 134
Hungarian Christmas Dessert (Mákos Guba) 136
Rice Pudding 137
Semolina Pudding 138
Vanilla Kifli 139
Hungarian Coconut Balls 140

DRINKS 141
Hungarian Horntail Cocktail 142
Béla Lugosi 143
Hungarian Spicy Berry Float 144

HUNGARIAN HOT CHOCOLATE...145

BLUEBERRY BASIL MOJITO 146

ÁRPÁD LIMO 147

BEACH PALINKA 148

HUNGARIAN SUMMER COCKTAIL 149

ONE LAST THING **156**

Why Hungarian Cuisine?

If you've tried the quintessential Hungarian dish - "Gullash or Goulash" before now, you're likely quite familiar with the traditional Hungarian flavors. Well, Gullash is just the tip of the iceberg. You'll actually be surprised when you find other authentic Hungarian meals. This cuisine is one of the famous ones from Central Europe. The culinary culture of the Hungarian people is diverse and involves a variety of cooking techniques. In Hungary, you'll explore all sort of meaty treats, hot soups, and veggie rich stews.

In sum, Hungarian cuisine is originated from the nomadic lifestyle of the Magyar people. That lifestyle was heavily dependent on the lifestyle, which is why you'll notice several Hungarian recipes having beef, lamb, pork, and poultry. The use of dairy and eggs in the meals is also quite common in this cuisine because of the same reason. In addition to meats, some popularly used vegetables are grown in this region like bell peppers, a variety of chili peppers, and squashes. The culture of making stuffed food, whether it's the entrees, snacks, or dessert, is also quite common in Hungary. At some point in history, the Hungary basin was inhabited by Italians, Jews, Armenian, Saxons, Czechs, Poles, and Slovaks, and those traditions are heavily reflected in the Hungarian culture and cuisine. In fact, these influences have made this cuisine so diverse. Some of the commonly used ingredients in this cuisine include:

- Hungarian peppers
- Sweet paprika
- Dried herbs
- Horseradish
- Mustard
- Poppy seeds

Hungarian dishes are known for their unique taste and aromas. There are several dishes that are worth trying from this cuisine, such as:

- Goulash
- Chicken Paprikash
- Gundei Palacsinta
- Fisherman's soup
- Fozelek
- Dobos Torte
- Lángos
- Somloi Gulaska
- Stuffed Cabbage
- Csusza

In desserts and beverages, there are several good options to choose. The one that I personally like the most is the plum dumplings, so delightful in taste and mildly sweet.

Hungary

Hungary is located in Central Europe on the bank of the Carpathian Basin. On land, it shares borders with Slovakia, Ukraine, Romania, Serbia, Croatia, and Slovenia. Due to its geographic location, the place remained the center of many civilizations from Huns to Celts, Romans, Germanic tribes, Avars, West Slavs, and now Hungarians. For this reason, the contemporary culture in the country reflects the stark influences that those civilizations left behind. These influences make Hungarian culture so diverse and rich. And that's what I personally loved about the country.

Next, modern-day Hungary emerged when the Austro-Hungarian Empire broke into pieces after World War I. And after World War II, the country became the satellite state of the USSR. Hungary's tumultuous history also left a deep impact on its culture. Today, on the one hand, its historical places remind you of the great Austrian Empire and its landscape; on the other, its people tell the stories about the beauty of this land.

The country has a diverse landscape akin to its rich cuisine. Plus, a due to the varying altitude in the country, you'll get to experience the mountainous to the moderate climate. Besides the diverse climate, I was surprised and amazed by the biodiversity of the area. It's truly like a biodiversity hot spot. The area is inhabited by some of the rare breeds of animals and birds in the world. Its climatic, hydrological, and geological conditions are the major factors behind its diversity. The remote Hungarian hills are inhabited by several species of fauna and flora.

My love of the Hungarian cities and Hungarian cuisine was developed after visiting the country for several times. There I interacted with many people, especially those who were close to traditional food and cooking. I happened to make several friends there. Though one week wasn't enough to explore the entire Hungarian culture, it was adequate to learn about its different places, food, language, and people.

If you're planning to visit the country and explore its beauty and amazing landscape, then do try the five places that I personally visited and loved. The Great Synagogue, which is the largest synagogue in Europe, is a good place to visit. It was built back in 1859, and it can accommodate 3000 people. Budapest is a must-to-visit city. Since it's also the capital of the country, it gives you a beautiful view of the Buda Hills, which is just mesmerizing. Then Lake Balaton is a pretty sight to see. Szentendre, Heviz, Egee, Tihany, and Lake Beusiedle are some of the amazing and beautiful sites in the country that must be explored and visited once in a lifetime.

Breakfast

Hungarian Crepes (Magyar Palacsinta)

Preparation time: 15 minutes
Cook time: 15 minutes
Nutrition facts (per serving): 249 cal (5.3g fat, 4g protein, 0g fiber)

These Hungarian crepes are one healthy breakfast option that can be served with powdered sugar and chocolate toppings on the side.

Ingredients (5 servings)
2 large eggs
1 ½ cups milk
1 teaspoon pure vanilla extract
2 tablespoons butter, melted
1 cup all-purpose flour, sifted
2 tablespoons sugar
Dash of salt
2 tablespoons sunflower oil

Cottage Cheese Crepes
2 cups of cottage cheese
1 teaspoon cinnamon
A drizzle of maple syrup
An assortment of fresh berries
Icing sugar

Preparation

Beat the eggs with milk, vanilla extract, butter, all-purpose flour, sugar, and salt in a bowl. Set a griddle on low heat and add 1 tablespoon sunflower oil. Pour ¼ cup batter into the griddle and swirl the batter around, then cook for almost 1 minute per side. Cook more crepes using the remaining batter in the same way. Transfer the crepes to the working surface. Top the crepes with cottage cheese and cinnamon. Roll the crepes and transfer to a baking pan. Bake the crepes for 20 minutes at 275 degrees F in the oven. Garnish with maple syrup, berries, and sugar. Enjoy.

Paprika Tomatoes with Eggs (Shakshuka)

Preparation time: 15 minutes
Cook time: 15 minutes
Nutrition facts (per serving): 256 cal (5.2g fat, 23g protein, 18g fiber)

Have you tried Shakshuka for breakfast? Well, here's a Hungarian delight that adds eggs and tomatoes to your morning meal in a delicious way.

Ingredients (6 servings)
1 ½ teaspoon coriander seeds
1 teaspoon cumin seeds
1 ½ tablespoon hot paprika
½ teaspoons salt
3 large garlic cloves, peeled
1 large poblano chile, seeded and chopped
2 tablespoons olive oil
2 tablespoons tomato paste
1 ½ pound Roma tomatoes, halved lengthwise
4 large eggs
Black pepper, to taste

Preparation
Grind the cumin, coriander, ½ teaspoons, and paprika in a mortar with a pestle. Mix the garlic with the spice mixture in a bowl. Sauté the chile with 1 tablespoon oil in a skillet for 12 minutes. Stir in the spice mixture and tomato paste, and then cook for almost 1 minute. Add tomatoes and ¾ cup water, and then cook for almost 20 minutes.

Make 4 wells in this mixture and crack one egg into each well. Next, drizzle the black pepper and salt on top. Put on the lid and continue cooking for about 5 minutes until the eggs are set. Serve warm.

Hungarian Scrambled Eggs
(Magyaros Tojásrántotta)

Preparation time: 15 minutes
Cook time: 12 minutes
Nutrition facts (per serving): 213 cal (20g fat, 29g protein, 7g fiber)

The Hungarian scrambled eggs are famous for their delicious flavor and fluffy texture. Made from eggs and fresh veggies, this scramble pairs well with all types of bread.

Ingredients (8 servings)
8 eggs
6 bacon slices
1 onion, chopped
1 red bell pepper
2 tablespoons vegetable oil
Black pepper, to taste
4 crusty bread rolls

Preparation
Sauté the bacon in a skillet until crispy and transfer it to a plate. Add the oil and onion, then sauté until soft. Toss in the bell peppers, black pepper, and then sauté for 1 minute. Whisk eggs in a bowl and pour into the skillet. Cook the eggs for 2 minutes, then flip. Cook for almost another 2 minutes. Drizzle the bacon on top and serve warm.

Potato and Sausage Casserole (Rakottkrumpli)

Preparation time: 10 minutes
Cook time: 65 minutes
Nutrition facts (per serving): 478 cal (16g fat, 24g protein, 2g fiber)

This potato and sausage casserole tastes heavenly when cooked and baked at home. Serve warm with your favorite toppings on the side.

Ingredients (6 servings)
2 pounds (1 kg) of potatoes, unpeeled and scrubbed
6 hard-boiled eggs
8 ounces sausage
1 ⅔ cups sour cream
1 teaspoon salt

Preparation
Boil the potatoes in boiling water for 20 minutes until soft. Drain and allow the potatoes to cool. Peel and slice them into ½ inch rounds. Peel the eggs and slice them. At 350 degrees F, preheat your oven. Grease 1 ½ quart baking dish with butter and spread the potatoes slice. Add sour cream sausage, salt, and eggs on top. Bake the potatoes casserole for 45 minutes. Slice and serve.

Hungarian Mushroom Omelet

Preparation time: 15 minutes
Cook time: 25 minutes
Nutrition facts (per serving): 256 cal (16g fat, 19g protein, 6g fiber)

Here's another nutritious yet simple meal for the breakfast table. It has lots of nutrients and fibers to the table, along with healthy ingredients that are cooked together in a tempting combination.

Ingredients (6 servings)
5 tablespoons butter
1 onion, chopped
1 cup mushroom, sliced
6 eggs, beaten
½ teaspoon salt
½ teaspoon black pepper
½ teaspoon sweet Hungarian paprika

Preparation
Sauté the onion with butter in a large suitable skillet for 10 minutes until golden brown. Toss in the paprika and mushrooms, then sauté for 5 minutes. Whisk the eggs with black pepper and salt in a bowl. Pour this mixture into the skillet and cook for almost 10 minutes on low heat. Slice and serve warm.

Hungarian Omelet

Preparation time: 15 minutes
Cook time: 9 minutes
Nutrition facts (per serving): 410 cal (6g fat, 20g protein, 1.4g fiber)

Try this Hungarian omelet for your breakfast, and you'll forget about the rest. The recipe is simple and gives you lots of nutrients in one place.

Ingredients (4 servings)
1 teaspoon olive oil
1 small onion, sliced
¼ red bell peppers, deseeded, sliced
2 medium tomatoes, skinned, sliced
1 teaspoon paprika
2 large eggs, beaten
1 parsley leaf fresh, chopped
Salt, to taste

Preparation
Sauté the onions with oil in a skillet until soft. Stir in the bell peppers, tomatoes, and paprika, then sauté for 5 minutes. Beat the eggs with salt in a bowl. Pour this mixture into the skillet and cook for almost 2 minutes per side. Garnish with parsley leaves. Enjoy.

Potato Tofu Casserole

Preparation time: 10 minutes
Cook time: 65 minutes
Nutrition facts (per serving): 391 cal (33g fat, 29g protein, 2g fiber)

This iconic dish is known as the classic Hungarian breakfast, which is a good version of the basic potato casserole. Plus, it's super and simple to make.

Ingredients (6 servings)
2.2 pounds (1 kg) potatoes

Tofu Eggs
9 ounces firm tofu, diced
1 tablespoon black salt
2 tablespoons apple cider vinegar
1 cup of water

Sour Cream
2 cups of cashews, preferably soaked
1 lemon, juiced
1 tablespoon nutritional yeast
⅔ cup of water
Salt and black pepper, to taste

Sausage Crumble
2 onions, diced
1 can of kidney beans
2 tablespoons tomato paste
1 tablespoon hot paprika paste
2 teaspoons liquid smoke
1 tablespoon oregano
1 ½ teaspoons marjoram

1 ½ teaspoons smoked paprika
2 teaspoons garlic powder
½ teaspoons red pepper flakes
Salt and black pepper, to taste

Preparation
Add the potatoes to a pot filled with boiling water and boil them for 20 minutes. Drain and allow the potatoes to cool. Peel and slice the potatoes. Blend the lemon juice, yeast, water, black pepper, salt, and cashews in a blender until smooth. Mash the potatoes in a bowl with a masher. Sauté the sausage and onions in a skillet for 10 minutes and stir in the rest of the ingredients for the sausage crumble. Mix well and keep it aside. Cook the tofu with 1 cup water, black salt, and apple cider vinegar in a cookpot for 6 minutes, drain and crumble the tofu. Spread the potato mash in a casserole dish and then top it with cream and sausage crumbles. Bake the casserole for 30 minutes at 400 degrees F. Serve.

Hungarian Apple Pancakes
(Almás-Fahéjas Palacsinta)

Preparation time: 15 minutes
Cook time: 48 minutes
Nutrition facts (per serving): 226 cal (2.4g fat, 4g protein, 1g fiber)

Almas Palacsinta is one of the Hungarian specialties, and everyone must try this interesting combination of different apple and cream fillings.

Ingredients (12 servings)
3 cups flour
1 ½ cups mineral water
2 cups milk
3 medium-sized eggs
¼ cup oil
1 pinch salt
1 teaspoon cinnamon
2 medium-sized apples, cored and grated
3 tablespoons brown cane sugar

Preparation
Whisk the flour with milk, eggs, sugar, and water in a bowl. Set a griddle over medium-low heat. Add 1 tablespoon oil into the griddle and pour in 1/12 batter. Cook for almost 2 minutes per side. Make 12 pancakes using the remaining batter. Place the pancakes on a working surface before topping t them with apples, cinnamon, and sugar. Roll the pancakes and serve.

Hungarian Cauliflower Potato Casserole

Preparation time: 15 minutes
Cook time: 40 minutes
Nutrition facts (per serving): 471 cal (17g fat, 16g protein, 0.7g fiber)

This dish is the best way to enjoy a veggie mixed with eggs in a savory style. Serve the freshly cooked casserole with toasted bread.

Ingredients (8 servings)
8 ounces chorizo, chopped
18 ounces cauliflower
4 boiled eggs, peeled
14 ounces sour cream
1 tablespoon goose fat butter
2 ounces any yellow cheese
Salt and black pepper to taste

Preparation
Boil the cauliflower for 10 minutes in a cooking pot, then slices it. Whisk the sour cream with black pepper and salt in a bowl. Sauté the chorizo with goose fat in a skillet until crispy until brown. Stir in the sour cream, and then mix well. At 390 degrees F, preheat your oven. Spread the sour cream mixture in a casserole dish and then top it with the cauliflower, eggs, salt, black pepper, and cheese. Bake the casserole for 30 minutes until golden brown. Serve warm.

Pull-Apart Cake with Apricot Jam (Aranygaluska)

Preparation time: 10 minutes
Cook time: 30 minutes
Nutrition facts (per serving): 317 cal (14g fat, 9g protein, 0.3g fiber)

This pull apart is a perfect morning cake! Keep it ready in the refrigerator to serve with your favorite jam. It's super-rich, healthy, and delicious.

Ingredients (8 servings)
1 tablespoon active dry yeast
1 cup warm milk
½ cup and 2 tablespoons sugar
4 large eggs
Zest of 1 orange
1 teaspoon vanilla
1 cup 4 tablespoons unsalted butter
4 ½ cups all-purpose flour
1 teaspoon salt
1 ½ cups ground walnuts
6 tablespoons brown sugar
¾ teaspoon cinnamon
3 tablespoons cookie crumbs
¾ cup (50 g) apricot jam

Preparation
Whisk the yeast with warm milk in a large bowl and keep it aside for 5 minutes. Stir in the sugar, eggs, orange zest, vanilla, ½ butter, ½ cup white sugar, flour, and salt. Mix this mixture in a mixer until it makes a dough. Cover and leave it for 1 hour. Mix the remaining butter and white sugar, brown sugar cinnamon, cookie crumbs, and walnut in a bowl. At 350 degrees F, preheat your oven. Grease a 10-inch round pan with butter. Spread the dough into ½ inch thick

circle, then cut 1inch cookies out of it using a cookie cutter. Dip these dough bites into the butter mixture and then place them in the prepared pan. Cover and leave the dough bites in the pan for 30 minutes. Brush the jam on top and bake 40 minutes in the oven. Serve.

Hungarian Kifli

Preparation time: 15 minutes
Cook time: 12 minutes
Nutrition facts (per serving): 242 cal (8.4g fat, 5.2g protein, 1g fiber)

If you haven't tried the Hungarian Kifli before, then here comes a simple and easy to cook recipe that you cherish.

Ingredients (6 servings)

9 ounces cream cheese
1 cup butter
3 egg yolks
1 teaspoon vanilla extract
2½ cups all-purpose flour
1 pinch salt
½ teaspoon baking powder
3 egg whites
8 ounces ground walnuts
1 cup white sugar
⅓ cup confectioners' sugar for garnish

Preparation

Beat the cream cheese with butter in a bowl. Stir in the vanilla and egg yolks, then whisk well. Add the baking powder and flour before mixing until it makes smooth dough. Divide the dough into 5 portions. Place the portions in a plate and cover with plastic, then refrigerate overnight. Beat egg whites in a cooking pot until it makes soft peaks. Stir in walnut, then mix well. Spread the dough into a ⅛-inch-thick sheet and cut into 3-inch squares. Top the squares with ½ teaspoon of the filling. Fold the edges of the squares and pinch to seal the filling. Place these cookies on a baking sheet. At 350 degrees, preheat your oven. Bake the cookies for 12 minutes, then garnish with sugar. Serve.

Appetizers
and Snacks

Hungarian Nut Roll

Preparation time: 5 minutes
Cook time: 45 minutes
Nutrition facts (per serving): 231 cal (20g fat, 22g protein, 6g fiber)

This classic reflects one of the most delicious appetizers within this cuisine. You can try different variations for its toppings and sauces as well.

Ingredients (8 servings)
2 (¼ ounce) packages active dry yeast
Warm water, as required
¾ cup white sugar
½ cup shortening
1½ tablespoons shortening
½ cup butter, melted
5 egg yolks
1 egg
2 teaspoons vanilla-butternut flavoring
1 teaspoon ground nutmeg
1 teaspoon salt
8 cups all-purpose flour
2 cups warm milk
6 egg whites
8 cups chopped pecans
¾ cup white sugar
½ cup honey
1 teaspoon vanilla extract

Preparation
Mix the yeast with warm water in a bowl, and then leave it for 5 minutes. Stir in the sugar, egg yolks, butter, shortening, egg, nutmeg, salt, and vanilla-butternut flavoring in a mixing bowl. Beat this mixture with an electric mixer until creamy.

Stir in the yeast mixture, milk, and flour, then mix well until it makes dough. Cover and leave this dough for 1 hour, then divide the dough into 4 pieces. Beat the egg whites in a mixing bowl until it forms stiff peaks. Stir in the honey, vanilla extract, sugar, and pecans, and then mix well. Spread each dough piece into ¼ inch thick- 13x18 inch rectangle on a working surface. Top the dough rectangles with the pecan mixture and roll them. Place the rolls on a baking sheet and bake them for 45 minutes in the oven.

Pickled Sweet Peppers

Preparation time: 15 minutes
Cook time: 15 minutes
Nutrition facts (per serving): 113 cal (3g fat, 2g protein, 5g fiber)

You won't know until you try it! That's what people told me about these pickled sweet peppers, and they indeed tasted more unique and flavorsome than other pickles I've sampled!

Ingredients (6 servings)

5 large sweet red peppers, julienned
8 banana peppers, julienned
1 medium onion, sliced
8 garlic cloves, peeled
4 teaspoons canola oil
2 ½ cups water
2 ½ cups white vinegar
1 ¼ cups sugar
2 teaspoons canning salt

Preparation

Divide the peppers into 5- 1-pint jars and top them with oil, garlic, and onion. Boil water with salt, sugar, and vinegar in a saucepan. Pour this water into the jars and cover the lid. Place the jars in a cooking pot and be sure to pour in enough water to cover the jars. Put on the lid and continue cooking for about 15 minutes. Ensure that you allow the jars to cool. Serve.

Hunza Bread

Preparation time: 15 minutes
Cook time: 45 minutes
Nutrition facts (per serving): 230 cal (4.2g fat, 10g protein, 1.4g fiber)

If you haven't tried the Hunza bread before, then here comes a simple and easy to cook recipe that you can easily prepare and cook at home today!

Ingredients (8 servings)
3 (¼ ounce) packages active dry yeast
1 cup warm water
8 cups bread flour
1 ½ cups white sugar
2 teaspoons salt
6 egg yolks
1 cup margarine, melted
1 ½ cups warm milk
1 cup golden raisins
2 egg whites, beaten

Preparation
Whisk the yeast with warm water in a bowl and leave it for 10 minutes. Whisk the sugar, salt, and flour in a bowl. Stir in the yeast mixture, warm milk, egg yolks, and margarine, then mix well to make a soft dough. Knead the dough on a greased working surface for 6 minutes. Place the dough in a greased bowl, cover, and leave the dough for 1 hour. Add raisins to the dough and knead well. Divide the dough into 2 pieces and shape them into loaves. Place each loaf in a 9x5 inches loaf pan. Cover and leave the loaves for 40 minutes. At 350 degrees F, preheat the oven. Brush the loaves with egg whites and bake them for 45 minutes until golden brown. Serve.

Hungarian Fried Lángos

Preparation time: 15 minutes
Cook time: 20 minutes
Nutrition facts (per serving): 279 cal (5.2g fat, 2.8g protein, 3g fiber)

If you haven't tried this fried Lángos, then you must since they have no parallel in taste and texture.

Ingredients (4 servings)
1 large potato, freshly mashed
2 ½ teaspoons instant yeast
1 teaspoon sugar
1 ¾ cups all-purpose flour
1 tablespoon vegetable oil
¾ teaspoon salt
½ cup milk
Canola oil (for frying)
2 garlic cloves, halved
Salt to taste

Preparation
Mix the yeast with flour, sugar, potato, salt, milk, and vegetable oil in a mixing bowl until it makes smooth dough. Cover and leave this dough for 1 hour. Pour canola oil into a deep pan and heat it to 350 degrees F. divide the dough into 4 pieces and spread each piece into ¼ inches thick sheet. Deep fry the bread sheets in the oil until golden brown. Rub the bread with garlic and salt. Serve warm.

Hungarian Cheese Spread (Körözött)

Preparation time: 10 minutes
Nutrition facts (per serving): 231 cal (9.5g fat, 9.7g protein, 9g fiber)

Who doesn't like to a cheese spread? Cheese lovers can get ready to enjoy some heart-melting cheese spread on this menu.

Ingredients (12 servings)
1 small tub (8 ounces) large curd cottage cheese
1 smaller or ½ a large onion, grated
Small package (3 ounces) cottage cheese
1 onion, chopped
3 teaspoons paprika
½ teaspoons salt
½ teaspoons pepper
½ teaspoons caraway powder
1 cup red wine

Preparation
Blend the curd cottage, cottage cheese, paprika, salt, black pepper, red wine, and caraway powder in a blender. Stir in the onion and mix well. Serve.

Peanut Butter Bites

Preparation time: 15 minutes
Nutrition facts (per serving): 232 cal (11g fat, 13g protein, 3g fiber)

These peanut butter bites will satisfy your sweet cravings in no time. They're super quick to make if you have peanut butter and oats at home.

Ingredients (12 servings)
1 cup quick oats
½ cup peanut butter
¼ cup pure honey
¼ cup ground flaxseed
½ cup coconut, shredded
¼ cup sunflower seeds
Pinch of salt
1 teaspoon pure vanilla extract
3 tablespoons almond milk

Preparation
Mix the peanut butter with the remaining ingredients in a bowl, cover, and refrigerator for 3 hours. Divide the dough into small balls. Place the peanut butter on a tray with parchment paper. Refrigerate the snack bites for 1 hour and serve.

Hungarian Cheese Scones (Pogacsa)

Preparation time: 15 minutes
Cook time: 25 minutes
Nutrition facts (per serving): 196 cal (3g fat, 12g protein, 3g fiber)

Hungarian cheese scones are another Hungarian-inspired delight that you should definitely try. Serve with your favorite sauce.

Ingredients (8 servings)
21 ounce (600 g) plain flour
8 ounce (200 g) unsalted butter softened
⅔ cup (150 ml) sour cream
½ cup (100 ml) creme fraiche
1 teaspoon sugar
1 teaspoon salt
1 tablespoon instant yeast
2 eggs for the dough
1 egg for the egg wash
3 ½ ounces (100 g) Emmenthal cheese, grated

Preparation
Whisk the flour with sour cream, crème Fraiche, butter, sugar, salt, yeast, eggs, and cheese in a bowl until it makes smooth dough. Cover and refrigerate the dough for 2 hours. Knead the dough on a working surface and roll it into 1-inch-thick rolled dough. Cut a 2 inch in diameter cookie using a cutter. Cut the cookies in half into a scone. Place the scones on a baking sheet and brush them with egg wash, then drizzle the cheese on top. Bake the scones for 25 minutes in the oven at 350 degrees F. Serve warm.

Hungarian Stuffed Cabbage

Preparation time: 10 minutes
Cook time: 17 minutes
Nutrition facts (per serving): 101 cal (3g fat, 24g protein, 4g fiber)

What about the delicious stuffed cabbage rolls? If you haven't tried them before, now is the time to cook this delicious mix at home using simple and healthy ingredients.

Ingredients (6 servings)

1 large cabbage, about 4 pounds
1 egg
1 medium onion, chopped
1-pound lean ground beef
1-pound ground pork
½ cup converted rice
1 tablespoon Hungarian paprika
Salt and black pepper, to taste
2 cups sauerkraut
6 ounces tomato paste

Preparation

Parboil the cabbage leaves in a cooking pot filled with boiling water for 5 minutes, then drain. Transfer the leaves to a colander and leave them for 10 minutes. Meanwhile, sauté the onion in a greased skillet until soft. Stir in the beef, pork, paprika, salt, and black pepper, then sauté for 7 minutes. Stir in the tomato paste, rice, and egg, and then cook for almost 5 minutes. Place one cabbage leaf on the working surface and add 2 tablespoons filling at the center. Wrap the leaf around the filling to make a roll. Repeat the same steps with the remaining filling and cabbage leaves. Boil water in a cooking pot and place the cabbage rolls in the boiling water. Cover and cook the rolls for 5 minutes. Transfer them to a plate and serve warm.

Salads

Chalamade Cabbage Salad

Preparation time: 10 minutes
Nutrition facts (per serving): 127 cal (11g fat, 1g protein, 2.1g fiber)

Chalamade cabbage salad is the best salad to find in Hungarian cuisine. This salad is packed with nutrients as it's prepared with cabbage, carrots, and onion.

Ingredients (4 servings)

1 medium head of cabbage, shredded
1 large onion, sliced
2 medium carrots, grated
½ (16-ounce) jar of gherkins or pickles
½ cup distilled vinegar
¼ cup sugar

Preparation

Toss all the ingredients together in a salad bowl. Serve.

Hungarian Pepper, Tomato And Cucumber Salad

Preparation time: 15 minutes
Nutrition facts (per serving): 146 cal (11g fat, 9g protein, 4.1g fiber)

This tomato and cucumber salad is everyone's favorite go-to meal when it comes to serving. The good news is that you can prepare it in no time without any cooking.

Ingredients (4 servings)
4 large tomatoes, chopped
2 cucumbers, chopped
1 small red onion, chopped
3 Hungarian wax peppers, chopped
2 teaspoons fresh dill, chopped
1 garlic clove, minced
1 teaspoon sugar
¼ cup red wine vinegar
½ cup olive oil
½ teaspoons salt
½ teaspoons black pepper

Preparation
Toss all the tomato-cucumber salad ingredients together in a salad bowl. Serve.

Hungarian Salad

Preparation time: 10 minutes
Cook time: 10 minutes
Nutrition facts (per serving): 172 cal (5g fat, 1.4g protein, 2g fiber)

This Hungarian salad makes a great side for the table, and you can serve as a delicious and healthy snack meal as well.

Ingredients (4 servings)
3 ½ ounces (100 g) cauliflowers, chopped
½ cup (100 g) green beans, chopped
2 red and yellow peppers, chopped
3 ½ ounces (100 g) peas
½ head red onions, chopped
3 ½ ounces (100 g) carrots, chopped
2 ounces (60 g) olives, stuffed with peppers
2 tablespoons olive oil
2 tablespoons vinegar
4 garlic cloves
1 pinch black pepper

Preparation
Sauté the cauliflower, green beans, pepper, onions, and carrots with olive oil in a skillet for 5 minutes. Stir in the garlic, vinegar, black pepper, and olives. Sauté for 5 minutes. Serve.

Sour Cream Cucumber Salad
(Téjfélés Uborka Saláta)

Preparation time: 10 minutes
Nutrition facts (per serving): 56 cal (3.5g fat, 5.7g protein, 2g fiber)

The Hungarian sour cream cucumber salad is another most popular salad in Hungarian Cuisine, and it has this great taste from the special mix of paprika and cucumber.

Ingredients (4 servings)
2 cucumbers, sliced
1 teaspoon salt
1 tablespoon apple cider vinegar
1 tablespoon water
1 garlic clove, minced
1 small onion, sliced
¼ teaspoons black pepper
1 teaspoon Hungarian Red Paprika (sweet)
¼ teaspoons Hungarian Red Paprika (hot)
½ teaspoons sugar
¼ cup sour cream, full fat

Preparation
Whisk the sour cream with sugar, water, vinegar, salt, and black pepper in a salad bowl. Stir in the cucumber and rest of the ingredients, and then mix well. Serve.

Hungarian Olive Salad

Preparation time: 10 minutes
Cook time: 5 minutes
Nutrition facts (per serving): 211 cal (20g fat, 4g protein, 13g fiber)

The olive salad is the right fit to serve with all your Hungarian entrees. Here the olives and cauliflowers are mixed with veggies to make an amazing combination.

Ingredients (6 servings)
1 package (10 ounces) frozen mixed vegetables, thawed
1 cup fresh cauliflowers, chopped
¼ pimiento-stuffed olives, sliced
½ cup green onions, sliced
¼ cup canola oil
3 tablespoons white vinegar
1 teaspoon garlic salt
¼ teaspoon black pepper

Preparation
Sauté the cauliflower with canola oil and mixed veggies in a skillet for 5 minutes. Transfer to a salad a bowl and add the olives, garlic, black pepper, vinegar, and green onions. Mix well and serve.

Hungarian Cucumber Salad

Preparation time: 10 minutes
Nutrition facts (per serving): 253 cal (2g fat, 1g protein, 4g fiber)

This cucumber salad is a delicious and healthy salad, which has a refreshing taste due to the use of herbs and spices. It's great to serve with skewers and as a bread topping.

Ingredients (4 servings)
2 large seedless English cucumbers, sliced
1 onion, sliced thin
¼ cup chopped fresh dill
3 tablespoons white vinegar
3 tablespoons vegetable oil
1 teaspoon salt
½ teaspoon ground black pepper

Preparation
Toss all the cucumber salad ingredients together in a salad bowl. Serve.

Hungarian Chopped Salad

Preparation time: 10 minutes
Nutrition facts (per serving): 179 cal (16g fat, 5g protein, 3g fiber)

The Hungarian chopped salad is a special fresh veggie salad, and it's a must to accompany all the different entrees. Use this quick and simple recipe to get it ready in no time.

Ingredients (4 servings)
½ pound paprika salami, sliced
½ pound Havarti cheese, diced
2 cups white mushrooms, diced
2 Persian cucumbers, sliced
2 tomatoes, diced
2 Hungarian wax peppers, sliced
4 scallions, chopped
½ red onion, diced
2 tablespoons red wine vinegar
2 tablespoons cilantro, chopped
1 tablespoon sweet Hungarian paprika
1 teaspoon brown sugar
1 garlic clove, minced
1 teaspoon salt
½ teaspoon black pepper

Preparation
Toss all the chopped salad ingredients in a salad bowl. Serve.

Hungarian Potato Salad

Preparation time: 10 minutes
Nutrition facts (per serving): 276 cal (17g fat, 7g protein, 3g fiber)

It's almost if the Hungarian menu is incomplete without this roasted potato salad. It's made from potatoes and tomatoes, which add lots of nutritional value to this salad.

Ingredients (8 servings)
Roasted Potatoes
4 pounds baby red potatoes
¼ teaspoon smoked paprika
1 teaspoon salt
2 tablespoons olive oil
¼ teaspoon cayenne pepper

Salad
3 tablespoons sliced grape tomatoes
2 tablespoons fresh dill
¾ cup sliced onion

Vinaigrette
¼ cup olive oil
2 tablespoons mustard
2 garlic cloves minced
1 teaspoon smoked paprika
¼ teaspoon apple cider vinegar
1 teaspoon maple syrup

Preparation
Prepare the vinaigrette in a small bowl by mixing all its ingredients. Toss the potatoes with paprika, salt, oil and cayenne pepper in a baking tray. Roast those

potatoes in the oven at 450 degrees F for 40 minutes. Transfer the roasted potatoes to a salad bowl. Stir in the rest of the veggies and vinaigrette. Mix well and serve.

Hungarian Style Lettuce Salad

Preparation time: 10 minutes
Nutrition facts (per serving): 155 cal (8g fat, 13g protein, 2g fiber)

If you haven't tried the tossed lettuce salad before, then here comes a simple and easy to cook recipe that you can recreate at home for health and happiness.

Ingredients (2 servings)
½ cup white vinegar
½ cup of water
1 ½ tablespoon sugar
Salt and black pepper, to taste
1 head lettuce, torn in pieces
1 large cucumber, cut in quarters

Preparation
Toss all the lettuce salad ingredients together in a salad bowl. Serve.

Soups

Fisherman's Soup (Halaszle)

Preparation time: 10 minutes
Cook time: 1 hour 30 minutes
Nutrition facts (per serving): 425 cal (28g fat, 33g protein, 2g fiber)

Have you tried the Hungarian fisherman's soup before? Well, now you can enjoy this unique and unique combination at home.

Ingredients (6 servings)
2 whole perch, filleted, diced, head and bones
¼ cup olive oil
2 onions, chopped
1 green capsicum, chopped
3 tomatoes, peeled, chopped
2 tablespoons Hungarian sweet paprika
Sour cream, parsley, and white bread, to serve

Preparation
Sauté the fish heads and bones in 1 tablespoon oil in a cooking pot over medium heat for 2 minutes. Pour 13 cups of cold water on top and cook the fish on a simmer for 30 minutes. Strain the broth and discard the solids. Sauté the capsicum and onions with oil in a large saucepan for 4 minutes. Stir in the tomatoes and cook for almost 5 minutes. Add the paprika and cook for almost 1 minute, then add the stock. Put on the lid and continue cooking for about 40 minutes on a simmer. Add the black pepper, salt, and fish pieces, and then cook for almost 10 minutes. Garnish with parsley and sour cream. Serve warm.

Goose Giblet Stock

Preparation time: 10 minutes
Cook time: 2 hours
Nutrition facts (per serving): 367 cal (6g fat, 19g protein, 1.2g fiber)

Try this super tasty Hungarian goose stock to serve patients and to cook different meals, and you'll never stop having it, that's how heavenly the combination tastes.

Ingredients (12 servings)
Giblets and neck of 1 goose
1 onion, sliced in half
1 carrot, split lengthways
1 thick celery stick, cut into chunks
1 bay leaf
1 sprig thyme
6 black peppercorns
Salt

Preparation
Add the giblets, onion, and all the ingredients, along with 4 cups water, to a cooking pot. Put on the lid and continue cooking for about 2 hours on a simmer. Strain and serve warm.

Bean Soup a la Jokai (Jokai Bableves)

Preparation time: 10 minutes
Cook time: 20 minutes
Nutrition facts (per serving): 391 cal (7g fat, 27g protein, 2g fiber)

Try cooking a delicious bean soup with some unique combination of spices and beans at home to enjoy the best of the Hungarian flavors right now.

Ingredients (6 servings)
1 tablespoon lard
1 tablespoon parsley, chopped
2 tablespoons sour cream
½ pound pork ribs, smoked
1 celery knob, peeled, diced
½ tablespoon paprika
1 tablespoon flour, all-purpose
1 onion, peeled, chopped
1 garlic clove, mashed
Salt, to taste
½ pound pork sausage, smoked
¼ pound beans

Preparation
Add the pork ribs, beans, celery, and 2 quarts water to a cooking pot. Cook the mixture until the beans are done. Meanwhile, sauté the onion with lard in a skillet over low heat until soft. Stir in flour and parsley. Mix well until this roux turns golden. Add the garlic, paprika, and 1 cup water. Mix well with the beans mixture and the smoked sausage. Cook for almost 10 minutes on a simmer. Garnish with sour cream and salt. Mix well and serve warm.

Souses Soup (Korhelyleves)

Preparation time: 10 minutes
Cook time: 25 minutes
Nutrition facts (per serving): 457 cal (19g fat, 23g protein, 5g fiber)

Souses Soup is one delicious way to complete your Hungarian menu, so here's a recipe for a delicious meal.

Ingredients (4 servings)

1 onion, minced
2 tablespoons bacon drippings
½ pound sausage, smoked, sliced
3 tablespoons sour cream
Salt, to taste
1 tablespoon paprika
1-pound sauerkraut
2 tablespoons flour, all-purpose

Preparation

Squeeze the extra juices from the sauerkraut, and then transfer to a cooking pot. Pour in 2 quarts water and cook until the sauerkraut is soft. Meanwhile, sauté the bacon in a frying pan until crispy. Stir in the flour and sauté until brown. Stir in the onion and sauté for 5 minutes. Add paprika and 1 cup cold water. Mix well and pour in the softened sauerkraut. Then mix well and cook for almost 15 minutes. Stir in the sour cream with the salt. Finally, cook for almost 5 minutes. Serve warm.

Paloc Soup (Palócleves)

Preparation time: 10 minutes
Cook time: 45 minutes
Nutrition facts (per serving): 424 cal (16g fat, 19g protein, 14g fiber)

Let's make a Paloc Soup with these simple ingredients. Mix them together and then cook to achieve great flavors.

Ingredients (6 servings)
2.2 pounds (1 kg) lamb leg, meat and bones separated
3 ½ ounces (100 g) smoked bacon lardons
2 onions peeled roughly chopped
3 garlic cloves chopped
7 ounces (200 g) potatoes peeled and diced
7 ounces (200 g) green beans
2 carrot peeled and sliced
5 ½ ounces (150 g) sour cream
A few stems of fresh dill
2 tablespoons paprika
½ lemon juice
½ teaspoon ground cumin
3 bay leaves
1 tablespoon salt
A pinch of black pepper

Preparation
Sauté the bacon with oil in a skillet until crispy. Add the onion and sauté until golden brown. Dice the meat into cubes and add to the skillet. Sauté until brown, then add 2 cups of water, black pepper, salt, garlic, bay leaves, paprika, and ground cumin. Put on the lid and continue cooking for about 30 minutes on low heat. Add 1-liter water, carrots, and potatoes. Cook for almost 10 minutes. Stir in the green beans and cook for almost 5 minutes. Mix the sour

cream with flour in a bowl. Pour it into the soup and cook until it thickens. Garnish with chopped dill. Serve warm.

Hungarian Kohlrabi Soup (Karalabe Leves)

Preparation time: 15 minutes
Cook time: 38 minutes
Nutrition facts (per serving): 386 cal (11g fat, 32g protein, 3g fiber)

This kohlrabi soup is a must-have for every fancy dinner. Besides, with the help of this recipe, you can cook it in a jiffy!

Ingredients (6 servings)
2 tablespoons butter
1 medium onion, chopped
1-pound kohlrabi bulbs, peeled and chopped
2 ½ cups vegetable stock
2 ½ cups milk
1 bay leaf
Salt, to taste
Black pepper, to taste

Preparation
Sauté the onions with butter in a large pan for 10 minutes. Stir in the kohlrabi bulbs and sauté for 2 minutes. Stir in 2 ½ cups milk, 2 ½ cups vegetable stock, and 1 bay leaf. Boil this soup, cover, and cook for almost 25 minutes on low heat. Discard the bay leaf, and then puree the soup until smooth. Add the black pepper and salt, and then mix well. Serve warm.

Hungarian Kohlrabi Chicken Soup (Újházi)

Preparation time: 15 minutes
Cook time: 10 minutes
Nutrition facts (per serving): 319cal (14g fat, 9g protein, 7g fiber)

Hungarian kohlrabi chicken soup is one option to go for in dinner. Sure, it takes some time to get it ready, but it's a great taste is totally worth all the time and effort.

Ingredients (6 servings)
3 ⅓ (1 ½ kg) whole chicken skinned and jointed
3 ½ ounces (100 g) turnips, peeled and cut in 4
1 ⅔ ounces (50 g) kohlrabi, peeled and cut in 4
1 small green pepper, left whole
1 stick celery, cut in 3
1 ⅔ ounces (50 g) kale, not chopped
1 small onion, peeled
1 medium tomato, whole
2 medium carrots, peeled and cut in 3
3 ½ ounces (100 g) chestnut mushrooms, sliced
3 ½ ounces (100 g) asparagus cut into 1-inch length
5 ⅓ ounces (150 g) frozen peas
3 ½ ounces (100 g) cauliflower florets
1 ⅔ ounces (50 g) vermicelli pasta, broken up
2 tablespoons black peppercorns
2 garlic cloves, peeled and chopped
2 pinches saffron or safflower
Salt to taste
A handful of fresh parsley, very chopped

Preparation

Add the chicken and enough water to cover it in a cooking pot. Cook the water to a boil. Add saffron, pepper, and garlic to the tea infuser. Add the tea infuser, carrots, celery, turnips, onion, kohlrabi, green pepper, kale, salt, and tomato to the pot. Cook the soup for 10 minutes. Stir in the peas, cauliflower, asparagus, and mushrooms. Shred the chicken meat and remove the bones. Stir in the kale and vermicelli, garnish with parsley, and serve warm.

Hungarian Mushroom Soup

Preparation time: 10 minutes
Cook time: 45 minutes
Nutrition facts (per serving): 201 cal (14g fat, 9g protein, 3g fiber)

Let's have a rich and delicious combination of mushrooms with a creamy base in a soup. Try it with warm bread slices, and you'll simply love it!

Ingredients (4 servings)
4 tablespoons unsalted butter
2 cups chopped onions
1-pound fresh mushrooms, sliced
2 teaspoons dried dill weed
1 tablespoon paprika
1 tablespoon soy sauce
2 cups chicken broth
1 cup milk
3 tablespoons all-purpose flour
1 teaspoon salt
Black pepper to taste
2 teaspoons lemon juice
¼ cup chopped fresh parsley
½ cup sour cream

Preparation
Sauté the onions with butter in a cooking pot for 5 minutes. Stir in the mushrooms and sauté for 5 minutes. Add the paprika, soy sauce, dill, and broth, and then cook for almost 15 minutes on a simmer. Mix the flour with milk in a small bowl. Pour this mixture into the soup and cook for almost 15 minutes with occasional stirring. Add the sour cream, parsley, lemon juice, black pepper, and salt. Mix and cook on low heat for 5 minutes. Serve warm.

Hungarian Lentil Soup

Preparation time: 15 minutes
Cook time: 1 hour 5 minutes
Nutrition facts (per serving): 258 cal (6g fat, 14g protein, 0g fiber)

The Hungarian lentil soup is an entrée that you must serve at the winter dinner table. This recipe will add a lot of flavors, aromas, and colors to your menu.

Ingredients (4 servings)
1 tablespoon olive oil
1 large onion, cubed
½ teaspoon minced garlic
1 ½ carrots, diced
1 stalk celery, diced
2 ½ cup crushed tomatoes
¾ cup lentils, soaked, rinsed, and drained
¼ teaspoon salt
¼ teaspoon ground black pepper
⅓ cup white wine
1 bay leaf
4 cups chicken stock
½ sprig fresh parsley, chopped
¼ teaspoon paprika
3 tablespoons Parmesan cheese, grated

Preparation
Sauté the onions with oil in a stock pot until soft. Stir in the celery, carrots, paprika and garlic, then sauté for 5 minutes. Stir in the tomatoes, lentils, salt, black pepper, bay leaves, lentils, wine, and chicken stock. Boil the mixture, then cover and cook on medium-low heat for 1 hour. Garnish with Parmesan and parsley. Serve warm.

Hungarian Cherry Soup (Meggyleves)

Preparation time: 15 minutes
Cook time: 5 minutes
Nutrition facts (per serving): 378 cal (11g fat, 33g protein, 1.2g fiber)

The Hungarian cherry soup is here to complete your Hungarian menu. This meal can be served on all special occasions and festive celebrations.

Ingredients (4 servings)

2 (24 ounces) jars of pitted sour cherries
½ teaspoons salt
1 stick cinnamon
1 slice lemon
1 (8 ounces) container sour cream

Preparation

Boil the cherries with juices, salt, cinnamon stick, and lemon slice in a pan for 5 minutes. Discard the lemon and cinnamon stick and allow the soup to cool. Garnish with sour cream and serve.

Hungarian Chicken Soup (Húsleves)

Preparation time: 5 minutes
Cook time: 60 minutes
Nutrition facts (per serving): 376 cal (14g fat, 22g protein, 18g fiber)

This Hungarian chicken soup recipe will make your day with a delightful taste. Serve warm with your favorite bread.

Ingredients (6 servings)
1 chicken with skin, cut into pieces
1 chopped onion, chopped
1 tomato, chopped
½ head of cabbage, diced
½ head of cauliflower, diced
1 bunch of parsley
6 ½ cup water
10 peppercorns
1 bay leaf
Salt to taste
4 garlic cloves
1 green chili pepper

Preparation
Add the chicken and rest of the ingredients to a cooking pot, cover, and cook for almost 60 minutes on a simmer. Garnish with parsley. Serve warm.

Strawberry Soup

Preparation time: 10 minutes
Cook time: 12 minutes
Nutrition facts (per serving): 360 cal (23g fat, 3g protein, 1g fiber)

Try this Hungarian strawberry soup with your favorite berries on top. Adding a dollop of cream or yogurt will make it even richer in taste.

Ingredients (6 servings)
2 quarts fresh strawberries
½ cup water
5 tablespoons sugar
1 tablespoon all-purpose flour
1 teaspoon orange zest, grated
1 cup heavy whipping cream
Fresh mint and strawberries, to serve

Preparation
Place half of the strawberries in a bowl and mash them with a potato masher. Blend the remaining berries with water, sugar, flour, orange zest in a blender until smooth. Pour this soup into a saucepan and cook for almost 2 minutes. Stir in mashed strawberries, then reduce the heat and cook for almost 10 minutes with occasional stirring. Allow the soup to cool and garnish with cream and strawberries. Serve.

Ham Green Bean Soup

Preparation time: 15 minutes
Cook time: 50 minutes
Nutrition facts (per serving): 329 cal (25g fat, 16g protein, 4g fiber)

You can give this soup a try because it has a good and delicious combination of green beans, ham, and onions.

Ingredients (6 servings)
Beans
2 pounds fresh green beans, trimmed
48 ounces water
1 ½ pound smoked ham, cut into chunks
2 cubes chicken bouillon
½ teaspoon paprika
¼ teaspoon cayenne pepper

Soup
4 tablespoons butter
4 tablespoons flour
½ onion, diced
1 teaspoon dried minced onion
1 teaspoon paprika
½ teaspoon ground black pepper
¼ cup of water
1 ½ cups sour cream

Preparation
Boil the green beans with water in a large cooking pot. Stir in the cayenne, paprika, bouillon, and ham, then Put on the lid and continue cooking for about 30 minutes, then reduce the heat. Allow the mixture to cool. Sauté the flour with butter in a skillet until 5 minutes. Stir in the onions, then sauté for 8

minutes. Reduce its heat, add dried onions, and then cook for almost 3 minutes. Add the black pepper, water, and paprika, and then mix well. Add the sour cream and green beans, and then cook for almost 5 minutes. Serve warm.

Main Dishes

Hungarian Goulash

Preparation time: 10 minutes
Cook time: 9 hours 5 minutes
Nutrition facts (per serving): 343 cal (13g fat, 15g protein, 2g fiber)

Hungarian goulash is the first recipe that everyone tries to cook on this menu. It's made with lots of veggies, spices, and meats.

Ingredients (12 servings)
3 onions, chopped
2 carrots, chopped
2 green peppers, chopped
3 pounds beef stew meat
¾ teaspoon salt
¾ teaspoon pepper
2 tablespoons olive oil
1 ½ cups beef broth
¼ cup all-purpose flour
3 tablespoons paprika
2 tablespoons tomato paste
1 teaspoon caraway seeds
1 garlic clove, minced
Dash sugar
12 cups uncooked egg noodles
1 cup sour cream

Preparation
Sauté the carrots, green peppers, onion with oil in a slow cooker for 5 minutes. Stir in the meat, ½ teaspoon black pepper, and ½ teaspoon salt, then sauté until brown. Add the broth, flour, tomato, paprika, garlic, sugar, caraway seeds. Mix well, cover the lid, and cook for almost 9 hours on Low. Serve warm with noodles.

Chicken Paprikash

Preparation time: 15 minutes
Cook time: 49 minutes
Nutrition facts (per serving): 181 cal (5g fat, 7g protein, 6g fiber)

If you haven't tried this wonder before, then here comes a simple and easy to cook recipe to wow everyone.

Ingredients (12 servings)
2 broiler chickens, cut into 8 pieces
2 teaspoons salt
1 teaspoon black pepper
2 tablespoons peanut oil
2 onions, halved and sliced
2 garlic cloves, chopped
3 tablespoons all-purpose flour
1 tablespoon sweet Hungarian paprika
2 cups chicken broth
1 cup sour cream
Minced fresh parsley and sweet Hungarian paprika
Cooked noodles, optional

Preparation
Rub the chicken with black pepper and salt and sear it in a Dutch oven with peanut oil until brown. Stir in the onions and sauté for 8 minutes, and then add garlic. Sauté for 1 minute. Stir in the paprika and flour, then mix well and cook for almost 5 minutes. Pour broth into the Dutch oven. Cook for almost 8 minutes, then cover and simmer the mixture for 30 minutes. Add the sour cream, and then cook for almost 5 minutes. Garnish with paprika and parsley. Serve warm with noodles.

Sauerkraut Stuffed Cabbage

Preparation time: 15 minutes
Cook time: 27 minutes
Nutrition facts (per serving): 352 cal (13g fat, 24g protein, 1g fiber)

The Hungarian sauerkraut stuffed cabbage rolls are a delight to serve during winters. They're known for their comforting effects, and the meal offers a very energizing combination of ingredients.

Ingredients (6 servings)

1 head cabbage
1 can (16 ounces) sauerkraut
1 cup onion, chopped
2 garlic cloves, minced
¼ cup all-purpose flour
1 tablespoon Hungarian paprika
¼ teaspoon cayenne pepper
1 can (16 ounces) crushed tomatoes
1 cup beef broth
½ cup long-grain rice, cooked
1-pound ground turkey
2 tablespoons fresh parsley, chopped
1 teaspoon salt
½ teaspoon black pepper

Preparation

Add the cabbage leaves to a pot filled with boiling water and cook for almost 5 minutes. Drain and place the leaves aside. Sauté the onion with oil in a cooking pan until soft. Stir in the turkey, garlic, paprika, cayenne pepper, tomatoes, parsley, salt, tomatoes, and black pepper. Mix and cook this mixture until 7 minutes. Meanwhile, boil the rice in beef broth until soft in a cooking pot. Mix the rice with turkey mixture in a bowl. Divide the sauerkraut and beef mixture on top of each cabbage leaves. Fold and roll the leaves until it makes rolls. Place the rolls in a cooking pot and pour water on them. Put the cooking pot on medium heat and cook for almost 5 minutes. Serve warm.

Hungarian Short Ribs

Preparation time: 10 minutes
Cook time: 2 hours 15 minutes
Nutrition facts (per serving): 361 cal (14g fat, 26g protein, 2g fiber)

Enjoy these Hungarian short ribs recipe with mixed tomato flavors. Adding cream or sour cream on top provides a very strong taste to the ribs.

Ingredients (8 servings)
2 tablespoons canola oil
4 pounds bone-in beef short ribs
2 onions, sliced
1 can (15 ounces) tomato sauce
1 cup of water
¼ cup packed brown sugar
¼ cup vinegar
1 ½ teaspoons salt
1 ½ teaspoons ground mustard
1 ½ teaspoons Worcestershire sauce
¼ teaspoon paprika
Cooked wide egg noodles

Preparation
Sear the ribs with oil in a Dutch oven over medium-high heat until brown from both sides. Stir in the onions, then sauté until soft. Stir in the tomato sauce, water, brown sugar, vinegar, salt, mustard, Worcestershire sauce, and paprika in a saucepan. Put on the lid and continue cooking for about 2 ½ hours. Serve warm with paprika.

Hungarian-Style Green Beans

Preparation time: 10 minutes
Cook time: 15 minutes
Nutrition facts (per serving): 210 cal (11g fat, 2g protein, 6g fiber)

Make this Hungarian style green beans meal in no time and enjoy it with some garnish on top. Adding a drizzle of paprika on top makes it super tasty.

Ingredients (4 servings)
1 pound fresh green beans, trimmed
¼ cup butter, cubed
½ pound sliced fresh mushrooms
1 ½ teaspoons paprika
2 garlic cloves, minced
¾ teaspoon salt

Preparation
Steam the green beans in a steamer basket placed over boiling water. Cover the green beans and cook for almost 10 minutes. Sauté the mushrooms and paprika with butter in a skillet. Stir in the garlic and salt, and then mix well. Toss in the green beans, then sauté for 5 minutes. Serve.

Beef Paprikash with Fire-Roasted Tomatoes

Preparation time: 15 minutes
Cook time: 2 hours 15 minutes
Nutrition facts (per serving): 534 cal (21g fat, 33 protein, 12g fiber)

Beef paprikash is also quite famous in the region; in fact, and it's a must to try because of its nutritional content.

Ingredients (6 servings)
⅓ cup all-purpose flour
2 tablespoons sweet Hungarian paprika
1 ¼ teaspoons salt
2 pounds boneless beef chuck roast, diced
2 tablespoons canola oil
1 large onion, chopped
1 small sweet red pepper, chopped
2 cans (8 ounces) tomato sauce
1 can (14 ½ ounces) fire-roasted diced tomatoes, undrained
1 can (14 ½ ounces) beef broth
1 package (16 ounces) kluski or noodles, boiled
3 tablespoons butter
Minced fresh parsley, optional

Preparation
Whisk the flour with ½ teaspoon salt and 1 tablespoon paprika in a salad bowl. Toss in the beef, and then mix well to coat. Add 1 tablespoon oil to a Dutch oven and place it over medium heat. Sear the beef in the oil for 5 minutes per side until brown. Transfer the beef to a plate when it's brown. Stir in the pepper and onion, then sauté for 5 minutes. Add the broth, tomatoes, tomato sauce, 1 tablespoon paprika, and ¾ teaspoons salt. Cover and cook this mixture for 2 hours until beef is tender. Garnish with butter and parsley. Serve warm with noodles.

Grandma Schwartz's Rouladen

Preparation time: 10 minutes
Cook time: 8 hours
Nutrition facts (per serving): 388 cal (11g fat, 28g protein, 3g fiber)

This Rouladen is everything I was looking for. The beef, spices, and mushrooms make a complete package for a health enthusiast like me.

Ingredients (4 servings)
3 bacon strips, chopped
1 ½ pounds beef top round steak
2 tablespoons Dijon mustard
3 medium carrots, quartered lengthwise
6 dill pickle spears
¼ cup onion, finely chopped
1 cup fresh mushrooms, sliced
1 small parsnip, peeled and chopped
1 celery rib, chopped
1 can (10 ¾ ounces) cream of mushroom soup
⅓ cup dry red wine
2 tablespoons Worcestershire sauce
2 tablespoons fresh parsley, minced

Preparation
Sauté the bacon in a skillet until crispy, then transfer to a plate lined with a paper towel. Slice the steak into 6 pieces and pound the meat into ¼ inch thickness. Rub the top with mustard, and then add 2 carrot pieces, 1 pickle spear, and onion. Roll the steak and secure it with a toothpick. Sear the roll in the bacon fat until brown. Transfer these rolls to the slow cooker. Add bacon, celery, parsnip, mushrooms, Worcestershire sauce, wine, and soup. Cover the soup and cook for almost 8 hours. Garnish with parsley.

Butternut Goulash

Preparation time: 15 minutes
Cook time: 33 minutes
Nutrition facts (per serving): 496 cal (8g fat, 34g protein, 3g fiber)

If you haven't tried the butternut goulash before, then here comes a simple and easy to cook recipe that you can cherish.

Ingredients (8 servings)
2 tablespoons butter
1-pound lean ground beef
1 large red pepper, chopped
1 cup chopped onion
1 can (28 ounces) no-salt-added crushed tomatoes
1 ½ cups butternut squash, peeled and cut into ½ inch cubes
1 can (8 ounces) tomato sauce
1 cup beef broth
1 teaspoon salt
¾ teaspoon chili powder
¼ teaspoon cayenne pepper
⅛ teaspoon dried oregano
2 cups zucchini, chopped
Shredded cheddar cheese, optional

Preparation
Sauté the beef with butter in a Dutch oven over medium-high heat until brown. Stir in the onion, red pepper, and sauté for 8 minutes. Stir in the rest of the ingredients, except for the cheese, and cook for almost 25 minutes. Garnish with cheese and serve warm.

Kohlrabi and Egg Noodles

Preparation time: 15 minutes
Cook time: 27 minutes
Nutrition facts (per serving): 105 cal (4g fat, 3g protein, 2g fiber)

These kohlrabi and egg noodles are loved by all, young and adult. It's super simple and quick to make. This delight is great to serve at dinner tables.

Ingredients (8 servings)
4 cups egg noodles
2 tablespoons butter
3 cups kohlrabi, grated
Salt and ground black pepper to taste

Preparation
Boil the noodles in a cooking pot filled with salted water then cook until they are soft. Sauté the kohlrabi with butter in a skillet. Stir in black pepper and salt, then sauté for 10 minutes. Add the egg noodles and cook for almost 7 minutes. Serve warm.

Blazing Brisket

Preparation time: 5 minutes
Cook time: 4 hours
Nutrition facts (per serving): 802 cal (4g fat, 19g protein, 1.7g fiber)

Try the blazing brisket at the dinner as the fish is infused with an amazing blend of Hungarian spices. Serve warm with your favorite sauces.

Ingredients (4 servings)

2 ½ pounds beef brisket
1-pound bacon, sliced
2 ½ cups brewed coffee
2 tablespoon salt
½ cup butter
¼ cup garlic, minced
¼ cup shortening
½ pound fatback, sliced
1 sweet potato, quartered
½ cup olive oil
2 tablespoon horseradish

Preparation

Wrap the brisket with bacon and place it in a baking dish. Drizzle the salt on top and pour the coffee on top. Cover and marinate overnight in the refrigerator. Sauté the garlic with butter in a saucepan over low heat until golden brown. Spread the shortening in a baking tray, add sweet potatoes, marinated brisket and pour the garlic butter on top, then cover with a foil. Roast the roast and potatoes for 4 hours at 325 degrees F in the oven. Mix the horseradish with the oil in a saucepan and cook for almost ½ hour on low heat. Slice the baked brisket and serve with the sweet potatoes and horseradish. Enjoy.

Hungarian Lecso

Preparation time: 5 minutes
Cook time: 25 minutes
Nutrition facts (per serving): 415 cal (21.1g fat, 16g protein, 2g fiber)

This Hungarian Lecso is a typical Hungarian entree, which is a must on the Hungarian menu. It has this rich mix of spinach, eggs, and the bread that I love.

Ingredients (8 servings)
3 tablespoons olive oil
2 pounds green bell peppers, seeded and cubed
1 onion, diced
2 (14 ½ ounces) cans diced tomatoes
Salt and black pepper, to taste to taste
¼ cup paprika
6 eggs
4 slices rye bread

Preparation
Sauté the green peppers and onions with olive oil in a suitable skillet for 10 minutes on medium heat. Add the black pepper, paprika, salt, and tomatoes. Cook for almost 10 minutes. Beat the eggs in a bowl and pour into the skillet. Stir and cook for almost 5 minutes. Divide this mixture on top of rye bread and serve.

Hungarian Chopped Liver

Preparation time: 5 minutes
Cook time: 20 minutes
Nutrition facts (per serving): 520 cal (32g fat, 43g protein, 0g fiber)

Simple and easy to make, this recipe is a must to try on this menu. Hungarian chopped liver is a delight for the dinner table.

Ingredients (8 servings)
2 tablespoons vegetable oil
1 tablespoon unsalted butter
1 large white onion, chopped
2 pounds fresh chicken livers
6 hard-cooked eggs
1 small white onion, finely chopped
1 bunch green onions, chopped
2 tablespoons paprika
2 tablespoons fresh parsley, chopped
1 head romaine lettuce
2 sprigs fresh parsley
Salt and black pepper, to taste to taste

Preparation
Sauté the onion with oil in a large skillet until soft. Stir in the chicken livers and cook until brown. Transfer the mixture to a bowl and crumble the liver using a masher. Add the eggs, raw onion, and green onion. Mix well, and then add salt, paprika, black pepper, and parsley. Mix well and refrigerate for 2 hours. Serve on top of lettuce leaves and garnish with parsley.

Veal Paprikash

Preparation time: 5 minutes
Cook time: 53 minutes
Nutrition facts (per serving): 445 cal (21g fat, 60g protein, 4g fiber)

Veal paprikash is one of the traditional Hungarian entrées made with a blend of veal, paprika, and peppers.

Ingredients (6 servings)
2 tablespoons lard
4 tablespoons sweet Hungarian paprika
2 medium onions, sliced
½ sweet red bell pepper, cut into cubes
2 pounds boneless veal, cut into chunks
2 cups chicken broth
1 cup sour cream
Salt and ground black pepper to taste

Preparation
Sauté the onions, bell pepper, ½ of the paprika with lard in a Dutch oven for 3 minutes. Transfer it to a bowl. Add the veal and remaining paprika to the lard in the Dutch oven. Sauté for 5 minutes, then return the veggies to the Dutch oven. Pour in the broth, boil, and cover to cook for almost 45 minutes. Stir in the paprika, black pepper, and salt. Mix well and serve warm.

Hungarian Pork Chops

Preparation time: 5 minutes
Cook time: 70 minutes
Nutrition facts (per serving): 376 cal (25g fat, 19g protein, 0.8g fiber)

A perfect mix of pork chops with sour cream sauce is all that you need to expand your Hungarian menu. Simple and easy to make, this recipe is a staple.

Ingredients (4 servings)
4 pork chops
¼ cup all-purpose flour
1 cup sour cream
¼ cup dry sherry
¼ cup ketchup
1 teaspoon Worcestershire sauce
¼ teaspoon paprika
1 bay leaf
Salt and black pepper, to taste

Preparation
Rub the pork chops with black pepper and salt then coat with flour. Add the oil to a suitable skillet and sear the chops on medium heat until golden brown from both sides. Whisk the sour cream, paprika, Worcestershire sauce, ketchup, and bay leaf in a bowl. Pour this sauce over the pork chops, cover, and cook for almost 1 hour on low heat. Serve warm.

Cabbage Balushka

Preparation time: 15 minutes
Cook time: 16 minutes
Nutrition facts (per serving): 482 cal (19g fat, 14g protein, 2g fiber)

Do you want to enjoy egg noodles with a Hungarian twist? Then try this Hungarian cabbage Balushka recipe. You can serve it with your favorite dips and sauce.

Ingredients (4 servings)
1 (16 ounces) package egg noodles
½ cup butter
1 large onion, chopped
1 head cabbage, cored and chopped
Salt and ground black pepper to taste

Preparation
Boil the egg noodles in salted water in a large pot until soft, then drain. Sauté the onion with butter in a wok for 8 minutes. Stir in the onions and cabbage, and then sauté for 8 minutes. Add the noodles, black pepper, and salt. Next, mix well. Serve warm.

Hungarian Lamb Goulash

Preparation time: 15 minutes
Cook time: 1 hour 40 minutes
Nutrition facts (per serving): 934 cal (61g fat, 73g protein, 2g fiber)

The classic Hungarian lamb goulash is here to complete your Hungarian menu. This meal can be served on all special occasions and memorable celebrations.

Ingredients (6 servings)

3 tablespoons butter
2 pounds cubed lamb stew meat
1 pinch of caraway seeds
1-pound onion, sliced
2 teaspoons paprika
1 garlic clove, minced
1 tablespoon lemon zest
1 (6 ounces) can tomato paste
1 (10 ½ ounces) can beef consommé
1 (10 ounces) package broad egg noodles, cooked

Preparation

Sauté the meat, onion, caraway seeds, and paprika with butter in a large pot until the meat is brown and onion is translucent. Stir in the lemon zest and garlic, then sauté for 1 minute. Add the beef consommé and tomato paste. Put on the lid and continue cooking for about 1 ½ hours on a simmer. Boil the egg noodles in salted water in a cooking pot for 8 minutes, then drain. Serve the goulash with egg noodles.

Hungarian Egg Barley

Preparation time: 10 minutes
Cook time: 52 minutes
Nutrition facts (per serving): 281 cal (16g fat, 19g protein, 2g fiber)

Hungarian browned egg barley is here to add flavors to your dinner table, but this time with a mix of rice and milk. You can try it as an effortless morning pudding.

Ingredients (4 servings)
1 tablespoon butter
½ small onion, chopped
1 cup dry Hungarian egg barley
2 cups hot chicken broth

Preparation
Sauté the onion with butter in a saucepan until brown. Stir in barley and broth, and then boil. Cover and cook the barley for 20 minutes on a simmer. Serve warm.

Hungarian Noodle Dish

Preparation time: 15 minutes
Cook time: 4 hours
Nutrition facts (per serving): 365 cal (17g fat, 15g protein, 5.4g fiber)

It's about time to try some classic noodle dish on the menu and make it more diverse and flavorsome. Serve warm with your favorite herbs on top.

Ingredients (5 servings)
½ (16 ounces) package wide egg noodles
1 ½ cubes chicken bouillon
2 tablespoons water
½ (10 ⅔ ounces) can cream of mushroom soup
¼ cup chopped onion
1 tablespoon Worcestershire sauce
1 ½ teaspoons poppy seeds
⅛ teaspoon garlic powder
⅛ teaspoon hot pepper sauce
1 cup 1 tablespoon cottage cheese
1 cup sour cream
2 tablespoon Parmesan cheese, grated
½ pinch paprika

Preparation
Add the egg noodles to salted water in a pot and cook until soft. Drain and keep them aside. Mix the bouillon cubes with water in a slow cooker over medium heat until dissolved. Stir in the cream of mushroom soup, poppy seeds, hot pepper sauce, garlic powder, onion, and Worcestershire sauce. Drizzle the cheese and paprika on top. Next, add the lid and continue cooking for about 4 hours on High. Serve warm.

Hungarian Stew (Porkolt)

Preparation time: 10 minutes
Cook time: 1 hour 45 minutes
Nutrition facts (per serving): 323 cal (13g fat, 27g protein, 1.4g fiber)

Hungarian stew is here to make your meal special. You can always serve the stew with warm bread on the side.

Ingredients (6 servings)
2 ½ bacon slices, diced
1 large onion, diced
2 tablespoons Hungarian paprika
¾ teaspoon garlic powder
⅛ teaspoon ground black pepper
2 ½ pounds boneless pork chops, trimmed
½ large yellow bell pepper, seeded and diced
1 (14 ounces) can diced tomatoes, with liquid
⅓ cup beef broth
1 cup sour cream

Preparation
Sauté the bacon in a skillet for 10 minutes until crispy. Next, add the onions and sauté until soft. Add garlic powder, black pepper, and paprika. Mix well and transfer this mixture, except for the bacon drippings, into a stockpot. Sear the pork chops in the same skillet for 5 minutes per side until brown. Transfer the chops to a working surface, and then dice them. Sauté the bell pepper in a skillet until soft. Transfer the pork, bell pepper, beef broth, tomatoes with liquid to the stockpot, put on the lid and continue cooking for about 90 minutes on medium heat. Garnish with sour cream. Serve warm.

Budapest Chicken Paprikash

Preparation time: 15 minutes
Cook time: 1 hour 10 minutes
Nutrition facts (per serving): 541 cal (33g fat, 44g protein, 2g fiber)

This new version of chicken paprikash tastes amazing, and it's really simple and easy to cook. It's great for all chicken and tomato lovers.

Ingredients (4 servings)
2 tablespoons bacon grease
1 large onion, chopped
3 garlic cloves, chopped
¾ teaspoon salt
1 teaspoon crushed red pepper flakes
3 tablespoons paprika
1 (3 pounds) whole chicken, cut into pieces
1 cup of water
1 (14 ½ ounces) can diced tomatoes
2 tablespoons all-purpose flour
1 (8 ounces) container sour cream

Preparation
Sauté the bacon in a large skillet until crispy. Stir in the onion, red pepper flakes, salt, garlic, and paprika, then sauté until soft. Add the water and chicken pieces, then cover to cook for almost 1 hour on medium heat. Add the tomatoes, sour cream, and flour, then mix well and cook until the sauce thickens. Serve warm.

Pasta with Cottage Cheese (Turos Csusza)

Preparation time: 15 minutes
Cook time: 15 minutes
Nutrition facts (per serving): 438 cal (22g fat, 17g protein, 1g fiber)

Turos Csusza is always an easy way to add extra flavors and nutrients to your menu. Check out this recipe that you can make in just a few minutes.

Ingredients (8 servings)
1 (16 ounces) package egg noodles, boiled
3 ½ slices smoked bacon
2 cups sour cream
1 (12 ounces) container cottage cheese
Salt to taste

Preparation
At 350 degrees F, preheat your oven. Sauté the bacon in a skillet until crispy, and then crumble it. Mix the noodles with sour cream and cottage cheese in a bowl and spread it in a casserole dish. Drizzle the bacon and salt on top. Bake the noodles for 5 minutes in the oven. Serve warm.

Gulyas Leves

Preparation time: 15 minutes
Cook time: 25 minutes
Nutrition facts (per serving): 679 cal (13g fat, 25g protein, 3g fiber)

Here's a delicious and savory combination of carrots, potatoes, and noodles that you must add to your menu.

Ingredients (6 servings)

3 tablespoons olive oil
1 onion, chopped
2 tablespoons Hungarian sweet paprika
8 ounces textured vegetable protein
1 green bell pepper, chopped
5 cups vegetable broth
4 large potatoes, diced
2 large carrots, diced
1 tomato, chopped
½ teaspoon salt
½ teaspoon ground black pepper
2 tablespoons chopped fresh parsley
1 packet egg noodles

Preparations

Sauté the onions with oil in a skillet over medium heat until soft. Stir in green pepper, vegetable protein, and paprika, and then mix well. Stir in the broth, tomato, black pepper, ½ teaspoons salt, parsley, carrots, and potatoes, and then cook it to a boil. Cover and cook on medium heat until the potatoes are soft. Add the noodles to the soup and cook until noodles are soft. Serve warm.

Paprikash

Preparation time: 15 minutes
Cook time: 65 minutes
Nutrition facts (per serving): 244 cal (6g fat, 8g protein, 5g fiber)

If you haven't tried the paprikash recipe before, then here comes a simple and easy to cook recipe to recreate at home in no time with minimum efforts.

Ingredients (6 servings)
3 slices bacon
1 (3 pounds) whole chicken, cut into pieces
1 teaspoon salt
1 teaspoon ground black pepper
2 onions, diced
1 tablespoon paprika
1 teaspoon caraway seeds
4 potatoes, cut into large chunks
½ cup sour cream
¼ cup chopped fresh parsley
1 tablespoon garlic powder

Preparation
Sauté the bacon in a skillet over medium-high heat for 10 minutes, and then transfer it to a plate. Season the chicken pieces with black pepper and salt, and then add them to the skillet. Sauté for 10 minutes until brown. Add the onions and sauté for 10 minutes, and then reduce the heat. Add the caraway seeds and paprika, and then cover to cook for almost 30 minutes. Toss in the potatoes and cook for almost 30 minutes with continuous stirring. Stir in the garlic powder, parsley, bacon, and sour cream. Mix and cook for almost 5 minutes. Serve warm.

Hungarian Stuffed Peppers

Preparation time: 15 minutes
Cook time: 10 minutes
Nutrition facts (per serving): 336 cal (13g fat, 28g protein, 1.7g fiber)

A perfect mix of pork and beef filling inside the peppers is worth to try. Serve warm with your favorite side salad for the best taste.

Ingredients (6 servings)
4 bell peppers, multicolored
1 small onion, chopped
1-pound ground chuck
½ pound ground pork
½ cup rice, rinsed and parboiled
1 large egg, beaten
1 teaspoon sweet Hungarian paprika
1 teaspoon salt
½ teaspoon black pepper
1 garlic clove, chopped
2 (8-ounce) cans tomato sauce
1 teaspoon sugar

Preparation
Chop off the top of the peppers and remove the seeds from the pepper. Rub the inside and out with black pepper and salt. Mix the ground chuck with onion, parboiled rice, pork, egg, paprika, salt, garlic, and black pepper in a bowl. Divide this mixture into the peppers. Place the peppers in a slow cooker. Mix the tomato sauce with sugar and pour it over peppers. Put on the lid and continue cooking for about 10 hours on Low. Garnish with sour cream and serve warm.

Crumbed Potato Casserole

Preparation time: 15 minutes
Cook time: 35 minutes
Nutrition facts (per serving): 316 cal (7g fat, 24g protein, 12g fiber)

The Hungarian crumbed potato casserole is famous for its crispy texture, unique taste, and delectable aroma. So now you can bring those exotic flavors home by using this recipe.

Ingredients (8 servings)

4 ounces butter
½ cup breadcrumbs
8 medium potatoes, boiled, peeled and sliced
8 eggs, hard-cooked, peeled, and sliced
1 pound Hungarian sausage, cut ¼-inch thick
1 cup sour cream
Salt to taste
Black pepper to taste

Preparation

At 350 degrees F, preheat your oven. Grease a casserole dish with butter and add breadcrumbs. Spread the potatoes at the bottom, top them with eggs, black pepper, salt, and sour cream. Cover the dish with foil and then bake the casserole for 20 minutes in the oven. Remove the foil and bake for another 15 minutes. Serve warm.

Hungarian Pork Stew (Sertés Paprikás)

Preparation time: 15 minutes
Cook time: 50 minutes
Nutrition facts (per serving): 428 cal (17g fat, 11g protein, 8g fiber)

The refreshing pork stew always tastes great when you cook pork meat with onion, all together with spices and Vegeta.

Ingredients (4 servings)
2 pounds boneless pork chops, sliced
1 tablespoon salt
1 tablespoon pepper
½ cup flour
⅓ cup canola
4 large onions diced
3 tablespoons sweet paprika
1 tablespoon Vegeta, or vegetable granules
1 cup sour cream

Preparation
Rub the pork slices with black pepper and salt, and then coat them with flour. Add 1 tablespoon canola oil in a skillet and sear the pork slices until golden brown for 1 minute per side. Transfer the pork slices to a plate. Sauté the onion with the remaining canola oil in a large pot until brown. Then reduce the heat and add paprika. Stir in the pork slices and pour enough water to cover the pork. Put on the lid and continue cooking for about 45 minutes on a simmer. Stir in the sour cream, black pepper, salt, and Vegeta. Mix well and serve with egg noodles. Enjoy.

Hungarian Green Pea Stew

Preparation time: 15 minutes
Cook time: 15 minutes
Nutrition facts (per serving): 342 cal (17g fat, 38g protein, 0g fiber)

Are you in a mood to have green peas on the menu? Well, you can serve this green pea stew with a salad and rice.

Ingredients (6 servings)
1 ⅓ pound (600 g) fresh or frozen green peas
2 tablespoons vegetable oil
1 onion, chopped
3 garlic cloves, minced
3 tablespoons flour
1 ½ cups of plant milk
Salt and black pepper, to taste
Fresh parsley, chopped
Sweet paprika powder

Preparation
Sauté the onions, green peas, garlic with oil in a cooking pot until soft. Stir in the vegetable broth. Cook for almost 10 minutes with occasional stirring. Mix the milk with flour in a bowl. Pour this mixture into the pot and cook for almost 5 minutes until the mixture thickens. Add the paprika powder, black pepper, salt, and parsley. Serve warm.

Minced Beef Goulash

Preparation time: 15 minutes
Cook time: 15 minutes
Nutrition facts (per serving): 443 cal (16g fat, 23g protein, 0.6g fiber)

Hungarian minced beef goulash is great to complete your menu, and this one, in particular, is great to have on a nutritious diet.

Ingredients (4 servings)
1 pound (450 g) lean minced beef
5 ⅔ ounces (160 g) macaroni
2.2 pounds (1 kg) whole plum peeled tomatoes
2 teaspoons paprika
1 tablespoon chili powder
2 tablespoons onion, chopped
1 garlic clove, chopped
6 ounces (170 g) tomato puree

Preparation
Sauté the beef with cooking oil in a cooking pot until brown. Stir in the garlic, onions, tomatoes, chili powder, tomato puree, and macaroni. Pour enough water to cover the mixture and cook until the macaroni is tender. Mix well and serve warm.

Hungarian Braided White Bread

Preparation time: 15 minutes
Cook time: 70 minutes
Nutrition facts (per serving): 338 cal (20g fat, 3g protein, 3g fiber)

Now you can quickly make a flavorsome Hungarian braided white bread at home and serve it as a fancy meal for yourself and your guest.

Ingredients (6 servings)
1 (¼ ounce) package active dry yeast
1 ¾ cups warm milk
1 egg yolk
1 egg, beaten
2 tablespoons white sugar
2 teaspoons salt
5 cups all-purpose flour
1 tablespoon poppy seeds
1 egg, beaten

Preparation
Whisk the yeast with warm milk in a bowl and leave it for 15 minutes. Beat the egg with sugar, salt, egg yolks in a bowl. Stir in flour and yeast mixture, then mix well until it makes smooth dough. Knead this dough for 8 minutes, and then divide the dough into two parts. Shape the dough into a cylindrical loaf and dive the loaf in half. Roll each half in a rope and pinch the four ropes at one end. Braid this rope and fasten them at another end. Place the dough on a baking sheet, cover, and leave for 40 minutes. Brush the bread with beaten egg and drizzle poppy seeds. Bake the bread for 15 minutes at 400 degrees F. Reduce the heat to 350 degrees F. Bake for another 45 minutes. Serve warm.

Sweet Potato and Egg Casserole

Preparation time: 10 minutes
Cook time: 30 minutes
Nutrition facts (per serving): 378 cal (11g fat, 25g protein, 3g fiber)

If you haven't tried the sweet potato egg casserole before, then here comes a simple and easy to cook recipe to recreate at home in no time with minimum efforts.

Ingredients (8 servings)

6 potatoes, boiled, sliced
8 eggs, boiled, peeled, and sliced
Seasoning salt to taste
1 cup margarine
1 (16 ounces) container sour cream

Preparation

At 350 degrees F, preheat your oven. Spread the potatoes and eggs in a 9x13 inches casserole dish. Drizzle salt on top. Mix the margarine with sour cream in a cooking pot over medium heat. Pour this mixture over the potatoes and bake for 30 minutes in the oven. Serve warm.

Zucchini Squash with Dill (Tokfozelek)

Preparation time: 10 minutes
Cook time: 15 minutes
Nutrition facts (per serving): 396 cal (13g fat, 12g protein, 4g fiber)

Zucchini squash with sour cream is loved by all, as this soup makes your meal healthy.

Ingredients (6 servings)
6 zucchini squash, peeled and grated
1 tablespoon of salt
½ cup white vinegar
3 sprigs of fresh dill
1 very small onion, sliced
½ cup of sour cream
1 tablespoon Flour
1 ¾ tablespoons sugar

Preparation
Toss the zucchini shreds with dill, vinegar, and salt in a bowl, cover, and refrigerate overnight. Soak the zucchini in a pot filled with water. Stir in the onion slices and cook the mixture until the veggies are soft. Mix sour cream with flour. Pour this mixture into the zucchini soup. Mix well and serve warm.

Paprika Foie Gras on Toast (Paprikás Libamáj)

Preparation time: 10 minutes
Cook time: 19 minutes
Nutrition facts (per serving): 492 cal (13g fat, 39g protein, 0.5g fiber)

This foie Gras on toast make a flavorsome mix of meat with bread. You can serve them for your breakfast or as a delicious entrée.

Ingredients (4 servings)
1 (2 pounds) duck foie gras, lobes separated and trimmed
1/3 cup rendered duck fat
1 tablespoon sweet paprika
8 bread slices, toasted
Sea salt, for garnish
Salt and black pepper, to taste

Preparation
Rub the foie gras with black pepper and salt. Melt the duck fat in an 8 inches skillet over medium-high heat. Soak the foie gras in the skillet for 6 minutes until brown. Transfer them to a bowl. Add the paprika to the skillet, and then mix well. Pour the mixture over the foie gras. Leave for 5 minutes, and then slice into ¼ inches slices. Place the two slices of the foie gras on a piece of toast. Drizzle black pepper and salt on top. Serve warm.

Hunters' Stew (Vada's)

Preparation time: 10 minutes
Cook time: 2 hours 9 minutes
Nutrition facts (per serving): 359 cal (5 g fat, 33g protein, 1g fiber)

Count on Hunter's Stew to make your dinner extra special and surprise your loved one with the ultimate flavors.

Ingredients (8 servings)
2.2 pounds (1 kg) veal schnitzel
2 tablespoons vegetable oil
4 carrots, thickly sliced
1 parsnip, thickly sliced
1 large red onion, sliced
2 bay leaves
½ cup (125 ml) red wine
1 tablespoon Hungarian mustard
1 lemon, juiced
2 tablespoons white wine vinegar
1 teaspoon sugar
7 ounces (200 g) sour cream

Preparation
Rub the veal with salt and sear with 1 tablespoon oil in a cooking pan until brown. Add 1 tablespoon oil, bay leaves, onion, parsnip, and carrots, then sauté for 4 minutes. Pour in the wine, lemon juice, and enough water to cover the veal. Cover the pot and cook for almost 2 hours on low heat. Discard the bay leaves. Add the mustard, vinegar, and sugar, and then mix well. Add the sour cream, black pepper, and salt. Mix and cook for almost 5 minutes. Serve warm.

Schnitzel (Rántott Hús)

Preparation time: 10 minutes
Cook time: 10 minutes
Nutrition facts (per serving): 482 cal (13g fat, 29g protein, 6g fiber)

This schnitzel will melt your heart away with its epic flavors. This sauce is filled with different spices that you easy to get and cook.

Ingredients (4 servings)
4 chicken breasts
5 tablespoons coconut oil
3 eggs
1 cup flour
1 cup breadcrumbs
2 tablespoons water
Salt to taste

Preparation
Whisk the eggs in a bowl, mix flour with salt in one plate, and breadcrumbs in another plate. Rub the chicken with salt, then coat with flour, and dip in the eggs. Coat the chicken breasts with breadcrumbs. Add 1 tablespoon oil in a skillet and sear the crusted chicken for 5 minutes per side. Sear the remaining chicken breasts in the same manner. Serve warm.

Hungarian Pork Stew (Borsos Tokany)

Preparation time: 10 minutes
Cook time: 60 minutes
Nutrition facts (per serving): 794 cal (51g fat, 69g protein, 1g fiber)

If you haven't tried the Hungarian pork stew before, then here comes a simple and easy to cook recipe that you can recreate at home perfectly.

Ingredients (6 servings)
12 ounces pork collar
4 ½ ounces (125 g) bacon
½ cup (75 g) onion
3 garlic cloves
2 teaspoons black pepper
Salt to taste
1 cup (250 ml) water
3 tablespoons (45 g) sour cream
1 tablespoon flour

Preparation
Sauté the bacon in a cooking pot for 6 minutes until crispy. Stir in the onion and garlic and sauté for 5 minutes. Add the pork, black pepper, and salt, then sauté for 5 minutes. Stir in water and cook for almost 45 minutes on a simmer. Mix the sour cream with flour, then pour it into a pot and cook for almost 4 minutes. Serve warm.

Hungarian Paprika Rice

Preparation time: 15 minutes
Cook time: 45 minutes
Nutrition facts (per serving): 412 cal (9g fat, 13g protein, 0.5g fiber)

The famous paprika rice recipe is here to make your Hungarian cuisine extra special. Serve it with flatbreads for the best taste.

Ingredients (4 servings)
2 cups onions, chopped
3 cups long grain rice
3 tablespoons olive oil
2 tablespoons Hungarian sweet paprika
2 teaspoons garlic powder
2 teaspoons onion powder
6 cups chicken stock more if needed
Salt and pepper to taste

Preparation
Sauté the onion with oil in a cooking pan until soft. Stir in the rice and the rest of the ingredients. Next, bring the stock to a boil. Reduce its heat and cook for 35 to 40 minutes until the rice is soft. Serve warm.

Hungarian Tripe Stew (Pacal Porkolt)

Preparation time: 10 minutes
Cook time: 1 hour 46 minutes
Nutrition facts (per serving): 470 cal (12g fat, 24g protein, 6 g fiber)

This Hungarian tripe stew recipe has unique flavors due to its rich blend of shrimp with cream sauce. Serve warm with rice or bread.

Ingredients (6 servings)
2 pounds (1 kg) precooked tripe, sliced
2 onions big, chopped
4 garlic cloves, chopped
2 tablespoons sweet paprika powder
2 teaspoon pork fat
1 teaspoon ground black pepper
2 teaspoon salt
1 teaspoon cumin
1 tomato
2 chilies

Preparation
Sauté the onion with pork fat in a skillet until soft. Stir in the garlic and sauté until brown. Add the black pepper, cumin, salt, and tripe strips and mix well. Stir in the paprika powder and Hungarian paprika, then sauté for 1 minute. Add enough water to cover the tripe and cover to cook for almost 1 ½ hour. Adjust the seasoning with salt and add the tomato slices and chili pepper. Cook for almost 5 minutes. Serve warm.

Hungarian Paprika Potatoes (Paprikás Krumpli)

Preparation time: 10 minutes
Cook time: 36 minutes
Nutrition facts (per serving): 219 cal (12g fat, 2g protein, 1g fiber)

Best to serve at dinner, this paprika potato dish delivers an energizing meal. It's truly a Hungarian version of delicious hash potatoes.

Ingredients (6 servings)
2 tablespoons butter
2 tablespoons olive oil
1 large onion, diced
1 ½ tablespoons Hungarian paprika
6 large potatoes, diced
1 green pepper, diced
1 tomato, peeled and diced
Salt and black pepper, to taste, to taste

Preparation
Sauté the onion with butter and olive oil in a cooking pot for 5 minutes until soft. Stir in the paprika, potatoes, tomatoes, green pepper, black pepper, and salt, then sauté for 1 minute. Pour enough water into the pot to cover the potatoes. Cook the potatoes for 30 minutes until soft. Serve warm.

Rice Pilaf with Pork and Vegetables

Preparation time: 15 minutes
Cook time: 1 hour 10 minutes
Nutrition facts (per serving): 456 cal (15g fat, 26g protein, 0.7g fiber)

If you haven't tried the Hungarian rice pilaf, then here comes a simple and easy to cook recipe that you can serve today.

Ingredients (4 servings)
1 cup Jasmine rice
3 cups water
1 onion chopped
3 garlic cloves finely chopped
8 ounces mushrooms, chopped
8 ounces colored bell peppers, chopped
8 ounces frozen peas
2 tablespoons vegetable oil
16 ounces of pork meat, diced
salt and black pepper, to taste to taste
½ teaspoon of coriander powder
½ teaspoon of dried parsley
½ teaspoon of dried dill
½ teaspoon of nutmeg
Frozen corn, carrots, tomatoes, etc

Preparation
At 350 degrees F, preheat your oven. Sauté the meat with oil in a Dutch oven until brown. Stir in vegetables and sauté until soft. Cover the meat with 2 cups of water and add the remaining ingredients. Cover and place this Dutch oven in the oven, then cook for almost 1 hour. Remove the lid and bake for 10 minutes. Serve warm.

Meat Jelly Aspic (Kocsonya)

Preparation time: 15 minutes
Cook time: 5 hours
Nutrition facts (per serving): 349 cal (7g fat, 29g protein, 3g fiber)

If you want some new flavors in your meals, then this meat jelly aspic recipe is best to bring variety to the menu.

Ingredients (4 servings)
3-4 pig trotters (feet), sliced in half
2 ham hocks/pork knuckles, cut into smaller pieces
10 ½ ounces (300 g) fresh pork rind
2 carrots, peeled
2 onions, peeled
1 garlic, peeled
8 whole peppercorns
Salt to taste

Preparation
Add the pig trotter, carrot, onions, garlic, pork rind, peppercorns, and knuckles to a cooking pot and pour enough water to cover them. Boil and cook the meat for 5 hours on a simmer. Add salt and skim off the fat from the top. Strain the broth and keep the veggies aside. Allow the broth to cool. Add the veggies and pork to a large bowl and pour the broth over it. Cover it with foil and refrigerate overnight. Serve.

Hungarian Meatloaf
(Stefánia Szelet)

Preparation time: 5 minutes
Cook time: 1 hour 15 minutes
Nutrition facts (per serving): 131 cal (11g fat, 10g protein, 0.3g fiber)

Here's a special Hungarian meatloaf, which is great to serve at special dinners and memorable celebrations. The meatloaf is stuffed with whole eggs and then baked into a delicious meal.

Ingredients (8 servings)
4 large eggs, hard-boiled
1 ⅔ pounds pork mince
2 soft white bread rolls, torn up
2 medium eggs
½ cup whole milk
1 onion, peeled and chopped
2 tablespoons olive oil
2 tablespoons paprika
3 garlic cloves, peeled and grated
1 teaspoon black pepper
1 tablespoon salt
2 teaspoons parsley, chopped
1 egg wash

Preparation
At 350 degrees F, preheat your oven. Soak the bread in milk for 5 minutes, then drain and squeeze. Sauté the onions with oil in a skillet until soft. Mix the pork mince with onion, garlic, bread, paprika, salt, black pepper, parsley, and 2 eggs in a bowl with your hands. Spread half of this pork mixture into 4-inch-wide rectangle on a baking sheet. Place the boiled eggs at the center of the meat mixture and top with the remaining meat mixture. Shape it into a loaf and brush

the top with egg wash. Add a splash of water to a baking tray and cover the loaf with a foil. Bake it for 1 hour in the oven, then remove the foil and bake again for 15 minutes. Slice and serve.

Cholent

Preparation time: 15 minutes
Cook time: 16 hours
Nutrition facts (per serving): 411 cal (9g fat, 11g protein, 7g fiber)

When you can't think of anything to serve in the lunch or dinner, then this Hungarian cholent will help you to thoroughly enjoy the authentic Hungarian flavors.

Ingredients (6 servings)
2 ½ pounds red potatoes, peeled and halved
2 whole onions, chopped
2 ½ pounds beef stew meat, diced
2 marrow bones
1 cup dried lima beans
½ cup pearl barley
3 whole garlic cloves
½ teaspoons black pepper
1-quart chicken broth
1 tablespoon salt
1 ½ teaspoons paprika
1 ½ teaspoons turmeric
1 teaspoon cumin
¼ teaspoons cayenne pepper
1 kishke
Water

Preparation
Add the meat, beans, marrow bones, and the rest of the ingredients to a slow cooker. Cover the lid and cook for almost 16 hours on low heat. Serve warm.

Hungarian Flaky Scones

Preparation time: 10 minutes
Cook time: 20 minutes
Nutrition facts (per serving): 326 cal (17g fat, 14g protein, 1.2g fiber)

Here's another classic recipe for your dinner, lunch, or snack collection. Serve it with a delicious entree and enjoy the best of it.

Ingredients (12 servings)
4 teaspoons active dry yeast
3 tablespoons milk
1 pinch granulated sugar
⅓ cup sour cream
2 large egg yolks
2 ¼ cups all-purpose flour
3 tablespoons confectioners' sugar
½ teaspoon salt
½ cup (1 stick) unsalted butter, cut into ½-inch cubes, chilled
1 large egg, beaten
1 ½ tablespoons poppy seeds or sesame seeds

Preparation
Mix the yeast with warm milk in a large bowl and leave it for 5 minutes. Stir in the sugar, sour cream, egg yolks, sugar, salt, butter and flour in a bowl and mix until it makes smooth dough. Spread the dough on a working surface into a ½ inch thick sheet. Cut the sheet using a cookie cutter into a 3-inch cookie, and then cut them into half to get the scones. Place the scones on a baking sheet lined with parchment paper, brush them with the egg wash and drizzle poppy seeds on top. Drizzle cheese on top of the scones. Bake them for 20 minutes, then serve warm.

Desserts

Gerbeaud Cake

Preparation time: 10 minutes
Cook time: 31 minutes
Nutrition facts (per serving): 379 cal (11g fat, 34g protein, 3g fiber)

If you haven't tried the Hungarian Gerbeaud cake before, then here comes a simple and recipe to please everyone.

Ingredients (8 servings)
Dough
1 packet instant yeast
4 cups (500 g) all-purpose flour
½ cup of sugar
1 teaspoon baking powder
1 egg
7 ounces (200 g) butter, melted
½ cup milk

Filling
7 ounces (200 g) apricot preserves
7 ounces (200 g) walnuts, chopped
For the chocolate topping
5 ounces (140 g) dark chocolate
2 ounces butter

Preparation
Whisk the yeast with milk in a bowl and leave it for 5 minutes. Stir in the flour, sugar, baking powder, egg, and butter, then mix well until it makes smooth dough. Place the dough in a greased bowl and cover it with a plastic wrap. Leave the dough for 40 minutes. Mix the apricot with the walnuts in a bowl. At 355 degrees F, preheat your oven. Spread a parchment paper in a 13x9 inches baking pan. Cut the dough into 3 parts. Roll one dough piece into a 7 inches round.

Place this sheet in a greased 7 inches baking pan. Top it with ⅓ of the apricot mixture, and then repeat the same with the remaining dough and apricot mixture to make three layers. Bake the cake for 30 minutes until golden brown. Melt chocolate with butter in a bowl for 15 seconds by heating it in the microwave. Pour this chocolate over the cake and allow it to cool. Slice and serve.

Hungarian Cream Puffs

Preparation time: 15 minutes
Cook time: 23 minutes
Nutrition facts (per serving): 347 cal (5g fat, 7g protein, 5g fiber)

A dessert that has no parallel, the Hungarian cream puffs are made with cream cheese, flour, and egg batter, which give them a super soft and moist texture.

Ingredients (8 servings)
1 cup of water
4 ounces unsalted butter
⅛ teaspoon salt
1 cup all-purpose flour
4 large eggs
1 cup heavy cream, whipped
6 ounces semisweet chocolate, melted

Instructions
At 375 degrees F, preheat your oven. Layer a 12-muffin tray with cooking spray. Melt the butter in a pan and add salt and water. Stir in the flour, then mix and cook for almost 3 minutes. Stir in the eggs and mix well to make a smooth batter. Divide the batter into the muffin cups and bake them for 20 minutes. Allow the puffs to cool, then garnish with chocolate and cream. Serve.

Hungarian Cookie Bars

Preparation time: 15 minutes
Cook time: 40 minutes
Nutrition facts (per serving): 221 cal (3 g fat, 4 g protein, 2.8g fiber)

Yes, you can make something as delicious as these Hungarian cookie bars by using only basic dessert and cookie ingredients and some simple techniques.

Ingredients (12 servings)
1 ¾ cups brown sugar, packed
½ cup margarine softened
1 teaspoon vanilla
1 ¼ cups all-purpose flour
2 large eggs
1 cup chopped nuts

Preparation
At 325 degrees F, preheat your oven. Whisk ¾ sugar with margarine, vanilla, and flour in a bowl. Spread this mixture in a greased- 9 inches baking pan. Beat the eggs with 1 cup brown sugar in a bowl until fluffy. Spread the egg mixture on top of the crust and drizzle nuts on top. Bake the batter for 40 minutes at 325 degrees F. Cut the cake into bars and serve.

Hungarian Dobosh Torte

Preparation time: 15 minutes
Cook time: 7 minutes
Nutrition facts (per serving): 357 cal (12g fat, 5.5g protein, 1.4g fiber)

Try this Hungarian Dobosh torte on the menu. The sweet combination of cake with chocolate is bliss for all the sweet tooth fans like me.

Ingredients (12 servings)
Cake
8 ounces butter
1 cup of sugar
4 large eggs
1 ½ cups all-purpose flour
1 teaspoon vanilla extract

Filling
8 ounces semisweet chocolate, chopped
2 ounces unsweetened chocolate, chopped
1-pound butter, melted
5 large egg whites
1 cup of sugar

Caramel Glaze
⅔ cup sugar
⅓ cup water

Preparation
At 350 degrees F, preheat your oven. Beat the butter with sugar, eggs, flour, and vanilla extract in a bowl until it makes a smooth batter. Grease a 7 inch round pan with cooking spray. Spread the batter in a pan and bake for 7 minutes. Melt all the chocolate for the filling in a bowl by heating it in the microwave. Stir in

butter, and then mix well. Beat the egg whites with sugar in a bowl until fluffy. Add this mixture to the chocolate, and then mix gently. Slice the cake into 4 layers using a twine. Place one cake layer in a cake pan. Spread a layer of chocolate on top, repeat the layers. Mix the sugar and water in a saucepan to prepare the glaze. Cook the glaze until the sugar is caramelized. Pour this caramel on top of the cake. Allow the cake to cool and slice to serve.

Zserbo Szelet

Preparation time: 10 minutes
Cook time: 26 minutes
Nutrition facts (per serving): 425 cal (17g fat, 5g protein, 0.8g fiber)

This Hungarian Zserbo Szelet will leave you spellbound due to its mildly sweet taste and the unforgettable combination of apricot jam and walnuts.

Ingredients (12 servings)
Filling
1 ½ cups of walnuts
½ cup of sugar
1 cup apricot jam

Dough
¼ cup of warm milk
1 teaspoon yeast
2 cups all-purpose flour
¼ cup of sugar
1 teaspoon baking soda
¼ teaspoons salt
1 stick of unsalted butter
¼ cup sour cream
12 ounces chocolate chips

Preparation
Grind the walnuts with sugar and jam in a food processor until it makes a coarse meal. Mix the warm milk with yeast in a bowl, then leave for 5 minutes. Stir in the flour, sugar, baking soda, sour cream, salt, and butter to the yeast mixture. Mix well until it makes a smooth dough. Cover and leave the dough for 1 hour. Divide the dough in half. Spread each half into a ¼ inch thick sheet. Grease an 8 inches baking pan with butter and place the sheet in the pan. Top the sheet with

walnuts mixture. Place another dough sheet on top and bake for 25 minutes in the oven. Melt the chocolate chips in a bowl by heating them in the microwave. Drizzle chocolate on top of Szelet. Slice and serve.

Hungarian Apricot Kolaches

Preparation time: 15 minutes
Cook time: 12 minutes
Nutrition facts (per serving): 57 cal (4g fat, 1g protein, 4g fiber)

The famous apricot kolaches are essential to try on the Hungarian dessert menu. Try cooking them at home and savor them!

Ingredients (12 servings)
8 ounces cream cheese, softened
1 cup butter, softened
2 ¼ cups all-purpose flour
½ teaspoon salt
1 cup apricot preserves
¼ cup sanding sugar

Preparation
Beat the cream cheese with butter in a bowl until fluffy, and then stir in the salt and flour. Mix well and divide the dough into 4 equal portions. Layer a baking sheet with parchment paper. Spread each dough portion into a ⅛ inch thick sheet and cut into 2-inch squares. Add a tablespoon of apricot preserves at the center of each square. Bring in the corner of each square and pinch them together. Dust the cookies with sugar. Place them on a baking sheet, and then bake for 12 minutes until golden brown. Allow them to cool. Serve.

Chimney Cake

Preparation time: 10 minutes
Cook time: 10 minutes
Nutrition facts (per serving): 408 cal (20g fat, 34g protein, 0.4g fiber)

If you want something exotic on your dessert menu, then nothing can taste better than these delicious chimney cakes.

Ingredients (6 servings)
1 egg, beaten
4 egg yolks
3 cup water
4 pounds (2 kg) Flour
8 ⅔ ounces (¼ kg) Sugar
8 ⅔ ounces (¼ kg) Butter, melted
1 pinch salt
2 teaspoons of yeast
Sugar for coating

Preparation
Beat the egg, egg yolk, water, and rest of the ingredients in a bowl until it makes smooth dough. Divide the dough into 16 pieces. Spread each piece into a rectangle. Roll each rectangle, and then pinch the two opposite edges together. Dust these rolls with sugar and place them on a baking sheet. Bake them for 5-10 minutes until golden brown. Serve.

Hungarian Walnut Rolls

Preparation time: 10 minutes
Cook time: 14 minutes
Nutrition facts (per serving): 202 cal (7g fat, 6g protein, 1.3g fiber)

If you're a walnut lover, then this Hungarian dessert recipe is the right fit for you. Try this at home and cook in no time.

Ingredients (12 servings)
Pastry
2 ¼ cups all-purpose flour
½ teaspoon salt
8 ounces cream cheese
1 cup unsalted butter, softened
½ cup granulated sugar

Filling
½ pound freshly ground walnuts
1 cup of sugar
½ cup of boiled milk
⅛ cup butter, melted

Preparation
Mix the milk with walnuts, sugar, and butter in a saucepan and cook for almost 5 minutes. Mix the all-purpose flour with salt, cream cheese, butter, and sugar in a mixer until it makes a smooth dough. Cover and refrigerate the dough for 2 hours. Divide the dough into 4 parts. At 375 degrees F, preheat your oven. Spread each portion into a ⅛-inch-thick sheet. Cut each sheet into 16 small squares. Add ½ teaspoon walnut filling at one corner of each square. Roll each square from one corner to another, and then pinch both the side of the rolls. Place the rolls on a baking sheet and bake them for 14 minutes. Serve.

Hungarian Pastry

Preparation time: 10 minutes
Cook time: 30 minutes
Nutrition facts (per serving): 493 cal (18g g fat, 9g protein, 3g fiber)

The famous Hungarian pastry filled with jam is another special dessert on the Hungarian menu. Try baking it at home with these healthy ingredients and enjoy it.

Ingredients (8 servings)

2 eggs
1 jam
½ teaspoons baking powder
1 pinch baking soda
1 ½ cups flour
½ cup sugar
1 teaspoon vanilla
1 cup nuts, ground
¼-pound butter

Preparation

Beat butter with sugar in a bowl. Stir in egg and vanilla, and then mix well. Stir in soda, flour, and baking powder, and then mix well. Spread the dough in a shallow baking pan and top it with jam, ½ cup ground nuts, and 2 tablespoons sugar. Bake it for ½ hour at 325 degrees F. Slice and serve.

Hungarian Christmas Cake (Beigli)

Preparation time: 15 minutes
Cook time: 30 minutes
Nutrition facts (per serving): 201cal (6g fat, 4g protein, 0.6g fiber)

The Hungarian Beigli has no parallel. Specifically, this apricot filled cake roll has a delicious blend of fruit preserves and raisins inside.

Ingredients (12 servings)
½ cup (100 ml) of milk
1 ⅔ ounces (50 g) sugar
2 teaspoons (25 g) fresh yeast
1 pound (500 g) flour
7 ounces (200 g) butter
2 eggs

Walnut Filling
7 ounces (200 g) ground walnuts
5 ⅓ ounces (150 g) sugar
2 tablespoons apricot jam
⅓ cup of milk
½ cup raisins

Poppy seed filling
7 ounces (200 g) ground poppy seeds
5 ⅓ ounces (150 g) sugar
2 tablespoons apricot jam
75 ml of milk
½ cup (100 ml) raisins
Brush with egg
1 egg

Preparation

At 300 degrees F, preheat your oven. Whisk the yeast with the milk in a bowl and stir in the rest of the dough ingredients, then mix well until smooth. Knead the dough for 2 minutes, cover, and leave the dough for 1 hour. Mix all the ingredients for fillings in a saucepan and cook until it thickens. Divide the dough into two parts and spread each piece into a square. Top the squares with the filling and roll them. Brush them with the egg and place them on a baking sheet. Bake the rolls for 30 minutes at 392 degrees F. Slice and serve.

Plum Dumplings
(Szilvás Gombóc)

Preparation time: 10 minutes
Cook time: 30 minutes
Nutrition facts (per serving): 203 cal (7g fat, 3g protein, 1g fiber)

The Hungarian plum dumplings are great to serve with all the hot beverages, and they're popular for their highly sweet and earthy taste.

Ingredients (12 servings)
5 medium potatoes, peeled, boiled, mashed
2 large eggs
1 teaspoon salt
2 ½ cups all-purpose flour
18 damson or Italian prune plums, washed and pitted
4 tablespoons butter
1 ½ cups breadcrumbs
¼ cup sugar
1 tablespoon cinnamon

Preparation
Boil the potatoes in hot water for 25 minutes until soft. Mash the potatoes in a bowl. Stir in the eggs, salt and flour, then mix well. Cover and leave the dough for 30 minutes. Spread the dough into a ⅓-inch sheet and cut into 2 inches squares. Top them with plums and fold them in half. Crimp the edges and boil the dumplings in hot water for 30 minutes, then transfer to a plate. Sauté the breadcrumbs with butter in a skillet until golden brown. Mix cinnamon with sugar in a bowl. Serve the dumpling with crumbs and the cinnamon mixture on top. Enjoy.

Raspberry Cream Roulade (Malna Piskotatekercs)

Preparation time: 10 minutes
Cook time: 15 minutes
Nutrition facts (per serving): 58 cal (1.4g fat, 1g protein, 2g fiber)

These Hungarian cream roulades are worth the try as they taste so unique and exotic. This dessert is definitely a must on the Hungarian menu.

Ingredients (12 servings)
Sponge Cake
6 large eggs
1 pinch salt
1 tablespoon water
6 tablespoons sugar
4 tablespoons flour

Filling
1 (12-ounce) can raspberry filling
1 cup whipping cream
1 (8-ounce) package cream cheese
½ cup sugar, granulated
1 tablespoon vanilla
2 pints raspberries

Preparation
At 375 degrees F, preheat your oven. Beat the egg whites with 1 tablespoon water in a baking bowl until it makes stiff peaks. Stir in the egg yolks and beat for 2 minutes. Stir in the remaining dough ingredients, then mix well until it makes a smooth batter. Spread the batter in a greased rectangular baking pan and bake for 15 minutes, then allow it to cool. Remove the cake from the pan and transfer it to a working surface. Beat the cream with sugar, cream cheese,

and vanilla in a mixer until fluffy. Place the sponge cake on parchment paper. Top it with the cream cheese mixture and raspberries, and then roll the sponge cake. Wrap the cake roll into the parchment paper, then refrigerate for 1 hour. Slice the roll into thick slices and dust them with sugar. Serve.

Vanilla Custard Cake

Preparation time: 15 minutes
Cook time: 15 minutes
Nutrition facts (per serving): 289 cal (13g fat, 3g protein, 2g fiber)

If you haven't tried the Hungarian custard cake before, then here comes a simple and easy to cook recipe that you can recreate at home in no time with minimum efforts.

Ingredients (12 servings)

1 package puff pastry
3 ⅓ cup milk
¼ cup cornstarch
½ cup (60 g) all-purpose flour
¾ cup sugar
3 large eggs
¼ teaspoons (1 g) salt
2 teaspoons (10 g) vanilla extract
⅓ cup (80 g) whipping cream

Preparation

At 400 degrees F, preheat your oven. Spread the pastry sheet and cut it into two eight-inch squares. Place the squares in a baking sheet lined with parchment paper. Bake them for 15 minutes in the oven until golden brown. Prepare the custard and beat the egg whites with salt and ¼ cup sugar in a bowl until fluffy. Beat the yolks with ½ cup sugar, flour, cornstarch, and 1 cup milk in a bowl. Boil the remaining 2 cups of milk in a saucepan. Stir in the egg yolks into the saucepan and cook until the mixture thickens. Stir in the vanilla extract and then mix well. Remove it from the heat. Fold in the egg whites and ¼ cup sugar. Place one baked pastry sheet on a baking pan and top it with the custard and place other pastry sheets on top. Refrigerate for 4 hours, and then slice. Garnish with sugar. Slice and serve. Enjoy.

Apple Poppy Seed Pastry (Flódni)

Preparation time: 15 minutes
Cook time: 1 hour 43 minutes
Nutrition facts (per serving): 650 cal (36g fat, 12g protein, 0g fiber)

The famous apple poppy seed pastry is essential to try on the Hungarian dessert menu. Experiment by baking it at home with these healthy ingredients and enjoy it.

Ingredients (12 servings)
Dough
4 cups flour
½ teaspoons salt
2 tablespoons sugar
8 tablespoons unsalted butter, diced
5 egg yolks
¾ cup white wine

Filling
4 ounces dried apricots, minced
1 ½ cups poppy seeds
1 cup white wine
1 cup 2 tablespoons sugar
1/2 cup apricot jam
2 teaspoons ground cinnamon
⅛ teaspoons cloves, ground
4 large apples, peeled and grated

Chocolate mixture
6 ounces walnuts, finely chopped
2 ounces bittersweet chocolate, finely chopped
4 ounces pitted prunes, minced

Zest and juice of 1 lemon

4 tablespoons unsalted butter, melted

1 egg, beaten with 1 tablespoon water, for egg wash

Preparation

Mix all the ingredients for the dough in a stand mixer until it makes smooth dough. Cover the dough with plastic wrap and cook for almost 30 minutes. Meanwhile, mix the remaining ½ of the wine with 6 tablespoons sugar, walnuts, and chocolate in a saucepan, and then cook for almost 3 minutes. Mix the apricots with ½ cup wine, remaining sugar, and all the ingredients in a saucepan. Cook the mixture for 10 minutes. Soak the prunes in 1 ½ cups water for 18 minutes, then drain. Mash the prunes in a bowl and stir in the lemon juice and poppy seed filling, then mix well. Layer an 8 inches square pan with parchment paper. Divide the dough into six pieces and spread each piece into a ⅛ inch thick sheet. Place one sheet in the square pan and top it with ⅙ of the fillings, then repeat the dough and filling layers. Brush its top with the egg wash and bake for 1 hour in the oven. Allow the pastry to cool, and then slice into squares. Serve.

Hungarian Christmas Dessert (Mákos Guba)

Preparation time: 15 minutes
Cook time: 20 minutes
Nutrition facts (per serving): 228 cal (6g fat, 4g protein, 3g fiber)

Here's one good option to go for in the desserts. You can also keep them ready and stored and then use them instead as instant desserts.

Ingredients (8 servings)
3 baguettes
3 cups (700 ml) of milk
3 ½ ounces (100 g) ground poppy seeds
1 ounce sugar

Preparation
Dice the baguettes and keep them aside. Warm up the milk in a saucepan. Stir in the sugar and poppy seeds. Add bread cubes and mix well. Spread them on a baking sheet. Bake the bread for 20 minutes in the oven. Serve.

Rice Pudding

Preparation time: 10 minutes
Cook time: 80 minutes
Nutrition facts (per serving): 344 cal (20g fat, 8g protein, 2.5g fiber)

Without this rice pudding, it seems like the Hungarian dessert menu is incomplete. Try it with different variations of toppings.

Ingredients (6 servings)
3 cups half-and-half, light cream
½ cup arborio rice
¼ cup of sugar
4 teaspoons butter
1 vanilla bean, split
½ teaspoon salt
3 egg yolks
⅓ cup of sugar
3 egg whites

Preparation
Boil the rice with half and half, butter, salt, vanilla beans, and ¼ cup sugar in a saucepan. Add the lid and continue cooking for about 25 minutes on a simmer. Allow the pudding to cool for 45 minutes. Beat the egg yolks in a mixer for 5 minutes until pale. Stir in ⅓ cup sugar, and then beat until it thickens. Beat the egg whites in a bowl until fluffy. Add the egg whites, egg yolk to the rice pudding, and then mix well gently. Spread the rice pudding in a soufflé dish and place it in a baking tray. Pour water into a baking tray up to 1 inch and bake the pudding for 50 minutes. Allow it to cool and serve.

Semolina Pudding

Preparation time: 10 minutes
Cook time: 8 minutes
Nutrition facts (per serving): 241 cal (4g fat, 2g protein, 1.1g fiber)

Here comes a dessert that's most loved by all. The semolina pudding is not only served as a dessert, but it's also a famous breakfast in Hungary.

Ingredients (6 servings)
2 ½ cups milk
10 teaspoons semolina
1 tablespoon vanilla sugar
1 teaspoon ground cinnamon

Preparation
Boil the milk in a cooking pot over medium heat. Next, add the sugar, cinnamon, and semolina. Finally, cook for almost 2 minutes until it thickens. Serve.

Vanilla Kifli

Preparation time: 10 minutes
Cook time: 12 minutes
Nutrition facts (per serving): 162 cal (13g fat, 7.5g protein, 2g fiber)

If you can't think of anything to cook and make in a short time, then try this vanilla Kifli because it has great taste and texture.

Ingredients (6 servings)
¾ cup unsalted butter softened
½ cup white sugar
1 teaspoon vanilla extract
2 egg yolks
2 cups all-purpose flour
½ cup vanilla sugar
2 (1 ounce) squares semisweet chocolate, chopped

Preparation
Beat the butter with sugar in a mixing bowl. Stir in the vanilla, egg yolks, and flour, then mix well to make the dough. Cover the dough and leave it for 2 hours. At 375 degrees F, preheat your oven. Take 1 tablespoon dough and roll it into a ½ inch thick and 3 inches long rope. Bend the rope into a crescent. Repeat the same steps with the remaining dough. Place the crescents on a baking sheet and bake them for 12 minutes. Allow them to cool. Melt the chocolate in a bowl by heating in a microwave. Dip the tips of the crescent in the melted chocolate. Serve.

Hungarian Coconut Balls

Preparation time: 15 minutes
Nutrition facts (per serving): 206 cal (9g fat, 4g protein, 0.1g fiber)

The appetizing coconut balls make a great addition to the menu, and they look fabulous when served at the table.

Ingredients (12 servings)
1 ¼ cups mashed potatoes
1 ¼ cups confectioners' sugar
2 tablespoons unsweetened cocoa powder
¼ cup lemon juice
2 tablespoons rum flavored extract
½ cup raisins
1 ¼ cups flaked coconut
1 teaspoon lemon zest
¼ cup flaked coconut

Preparation
Soak the raisins in lemon juice and rum extract in a bowl. Mix the mashed potatoes with cocoa, sugar, raisins mixture, lemon zest, and ¼ cup coconut. Make small walnut-sized balls out of this mixture. Roll these balls in the coconut shreds. Serve.

Drinks

Hungarian Horntail Cocktail

Preparation time: 5 minutes
Cook time: 20 minutes
Nutrition facts (per serving): 112 cal (2g fat, 4 protein, 3g fiber)

Beat the heat and try the famous Hungarian horntail cocktail with the hints of ginger beer. The combination is super refreshing and healthy.

Ingredients (2 servings)
Simple spiced syrup
1 cup of sugar
1 cup of water
3 whole cardamom pods
5 whole cloves
5 whole allspice
2 whole star anise

Hungarian Horntail
2 ounces plum brandy
½-ouncessimple spiced syrup
Ginger beer, to fill the glass

Preparation
Mix all the simple syrup ingredients in a saucepan and cook for almost 5 minutes on medium-low heat. Leave it for 15 minutes, then strain and allow it to cool. Shake the brandy with spice syrup in a cocktail shaker and serve with ginger beer. Enjoy.

Béla Lugosi

Preparation time: 5 minutes
Nutrition facts (per serving): 103cal (7g fat, 3g protein, 1g fiber)

The Hungarian Bela Lugosi is loved by all due to its refreshing taste and sweet flavors. Serve it chilled for the best taste and an unforgettable flavor.

Ingredients (2 servings)
1 ounce white rum
½-ouncescherry brandy
½-ouncestriple sec
1 ½-ouncescherry juice
¼-ounce Domaine de Canton

Preparation
Shake the white rum, cherry brandy, triple sec, cherry juice, and canton in a cocktail share. Serve.

Hungarian Spicy Berry Float

Preparation time: 10 minutes
Nutrition facts (per serving): 217 cal (24g fat, 12g protein, 0g fiber)

The Hungarian berry float drink is great to serve on all the special occasions and dinner. It has these appealing and creamy cherry toppings.

Ingredients (4 servings)
Smoothie
6 ounces strawberries, chopped
6 ounces blueberries
3 ounces blackberries
1 banana
2 tablespoons honey
Dash sweet Hungarian paprika
Dash sea salt
3 teaspoons freshly squeezed lemon juice

Other
1 tablespoon dried cherries
1 tablespoon crystallized ginger pulverized
Dark chocolate curls
2 teaspoons liqueur
2 teaspoons vanilla extract
2 ounces heavy cream
3 scoops ice cream/gelato
1 small bottle of lime-flavored Perrier

Preparation
Blend all smoothie ingredients in a blender until smooth. Soak the dried cherries in water for 30 minutes, then drain. Serve the smoothie with cream, liquor, ice cream, Perrier, chocolate curls, and cherries on top. Enjoy.

Hungarian Hot Chocolate

Preparation time: 10 minutes
Cook time: 8 minutes
Nutrition facts (per serving): 142 cal (13g fat, 6.3g protein, 1g fiber)

The Hungarian hot chocolate is famous for its blend of cinnamon and star anise, with milk and chocolate. You can prep this drink easily at home.

Ingredients (2 servings)
10 tablespoons powder chocolate
4 cups milk
2 pinches cinnamon
1 pinch anise
Chantilly cream, to decorate
Chocolate, grated

Preparation
Warm up the milk in a saucepan, then the anise, the cinnamon, and the chocolate. Mix and cook for almost 3 minutes. Garnish with cream and chocolate. Serve.

Blueberry Basil Mojito

Preparation time: 5 minutes
Nutrition facts (per serving): 156 cal (0g fat, 0.7g protein, 1.4g fiber)

The basil mojito is all that you need to celebrate the holidays. Keep the drink ready in your refrigerator for quick serving.

Ingredients (2 serving)
8 large blueberries
3 basil leaves
3 mint leaves
1 ½ ounces lime juice
1 ½ ounces rum
¾-ounces simple syrup
Club soda

Preparation
Shake the rum, simple syrup, club soda, mint leaves, lime juice, and basil leaves in a cocktail shaker. Serve with blueberries. Enjoy.

Árpád Limo

Preparation time: 5 minutes
Nutrition facts (per serving): 110 cal (0g fat, 0g protein, 1g fiber)

Here's a special Hungarian drink made out of apple and lemon juices with palinka, which is great to serve at special dinners and memorable celebrations.

Ingredients (2 servings)

1 ⅓ ounces of apple palinka
1 bar spoon of sugar
Juice and zest of 2 lemons
1 ⅓ ounces of apple juice
1 ⅓ ounces of soda ice

Preparation

Mix the apple palinka, sugar, lemon juice, apple juice, and soda ice in a cocktail shaker. Garnish with lemon slices. Serve.

Beach Palinka

Preparation time: 5 minutes
Nutrition facts (per serving): 122 cal (13g fat, 12g protein, 2.3g fiber)

Made from peach palinka, this beverage is a refreshing addition to the Hungarian cocktail menu.

Ingredients (4 servings)
1 ⅓ tablespoon of peach palinka
7 tablespoons of orange juice
2 ⅔ tablespoons of cranberry juice
Orange slices
Maraschino cherry, to garnish
Ice

Preparation
Blend all palinka, orange juice, and ice in a cocktail shake and serve with orange slices and cherry on top. Enjoy.

Hungarian Summer Cocktail

Preparation time: 1 minutes
Nutrition facts (per serving): 321 cal (20g fat, 24g protein, 0g fiber)

This refreshing cocktail is always a delight to serve at parties. Now you can make it easily at home by using the following simple ingredients.

Ingredients (2 servings)
1 ½ shot Tokaji Hungarian wine
1 shot Vodka
1 shot of orange juice
1 dash vanilla extract

Preparation
Shake all the ingredients in a cocktail shaker, and then serve.

If you liked Hungarian recipes, discover to how cook DELICIOUS recipes from neighboring **Balkan** countries!

Within these pages, you'll learn 35 authentic recipes from a Balkan cook. These aren't ordinary recipes you'd find on the Internet, but recipes that were closely guarded by our Balkan mothers and passed down from generation to generation.

Main Dishes, Appetizers, and Desserts included!

If you want to learn how to make Croatian green peas stew, and 32 other authentic Balkan recipes, then start with our book!

Order at www.balkanfood.org/cook-books/ for only $2,99

If you're a **Mediterranean** dieter who wants to know the secrets of the Mediterranean diet, dieting, and cooking, then you're about to discover how to master cooking meals on a Mediterranean diet right now!

In fact, if you want to know how to make Mediterranean food, then this new e-book - "The 30-minute Mediterranean diet" - gives you the answers to many important questions and challenges every Mediterranean dieter faces, including:

- How can I succeed with a Mediterranean diet?
- What kind of recipes can I make?
- What are the key principles to this type of diet?
- What are the suggested weekly menus for this diet?
- Are there any cheat items I can make?

... and more!

If you're serious about cooking meals on a Mediterranean diet and you really want to know how to make Mediterranean food, then you need to grab a copy of "The 30-minute Mediterranean diet" right now.
Prepare 111 recipes with several ingredients in less than 30 minutes!

Order at www.balkanfood.org/cook-books/ for only $2,99

What could be better than a home-cooked meal? Maybe only a **Greek** homemade meal.

Do not get discouraged if you have no Greek roots or friends. Now you can make a Greek food feast in your kitchen.

This ultimate Greek cookbook offers you 111 best dishes of this cuisine! From more famous gyros to more exotic *Kota Kapama* this cookbook keeps it easy and affordable.

All the ingredients necessary are wholesome and widely accessible.
The author's picks are as flavorful as they are healthy. The dishes described in this cookbook are "what Greek mothers have made for decades."

Full of well-balanced and nutritious meals, this handy cookbook includes many vegan options. Discover a plethora of benefits of Mediterranean cuisine, and you may fall in love with cooking at home.

Inspired by a real food lover, this collection of delicious recipes will taste buds utterly satisfied.

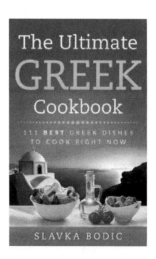

Order at www.balkanfood.org/cook-books/ for only $2,99

Maybe to try exotic **Syrian** cuisine?

From succulent *sarma*, soups, warm and cold salads to delectable desserts, the plethora of flavors will satisfy the most jaded foodie. Have a taste of a new culture with this **traditional Syrian cookbook**.

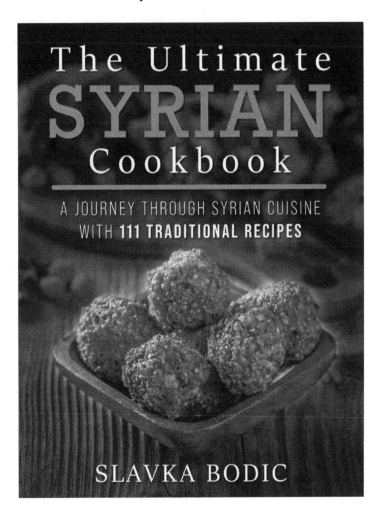

The Ultimate
SYRIAN
Cookbook

A JOURNEY THROUGH SYRIAN CUISINE
WITH **111 TRADITIONAL RECIPES**

SLAVKA BODIC

Order at www.balkanfood.org/cook-books/ for only $2,99

Maybe **Polish** cuisine?

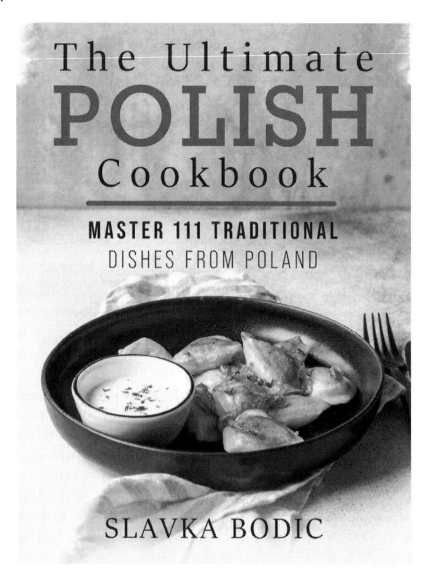

Order at www.balkanfood.org/cook-books/ for only $2,99

Or **Peruvian**?

Order at www.balkanfood.org/cook-books/ for only $2,99

ONE LAST THING

If you enjoyed this book or found it useful, I'd be very grateful if you could find the time to post a short review on Amazon. Your support really does make a difference and I read all the reviews personally, so I can get your feedback and make this book even better.

Thanks again for your support!

Please send me your feedback at

www.balkanfood.org